501
Practical
*L*ways to
*L*ove
your
Husband
& Kids

501

Practical

Ways to

Love

your

Husband

& Kids

By Jennifer Baker

CPH
SAINT LOUIS

To my husband, Paul, and to our children, Andrew
and Miriam. You have given me many wonderful
opportunities to love in practical ways.

Scripture quotations marked KJV are from the King James or Authorized Version of
the Bible.

Scripture quotations marked NKJV are from the New King James edition, copyright
© 1979, 1980, 1982.

All Scripture quotations, unless otherwise noted, are taken from the HOLY BIBLE, NEW
INTERNATIONAL VERSION®. NIV®. Copyright © 1973, 1978, 1984 by International Bible
Society. Used by permission of Zondervan Publishing House. All rights reserved.

Copyright © 1996 Concordia Publishing House
3558 S. Jefferson Avenue, St. Louis, MO 63118-3968
Manufactured in the United States of America

1 2 3 4 5 6 7 8 9 10   05 04 03 02 01 00 99 98 97 96

I would like to express my deepest thanks
to the following people:

To my parents, Jack and Lois Haas, whose love for me
and my family has been the source of much inspiration
for this book. Truly, I could not have done it without them.

To Jan Ferry, Peggy Piske, and Terri Reeverts
for the hours they spent reading the manuscript
and for the many helpful comments they made.

To Roger Sonnenberg for having the faith
to include me in this project.

To Ruth Geisler, my editor, for her
encouragement and expertise.

CONTENTS

INTRODUCTION

As I began to plan this book, I saw a need for parents, particularly wives and mothers, to have an easy-to-use handbook with ideas on a variety of subjects and situations—something that could be referred to a few pages at a time as the circumstance arose. The chapters are framed around the 12 months of the year, but ideas are not tied to specific calendar dates or events. Feel free to work through the book, beginning to end, or pick and choose ideas as you need them.

In my work as a marriage and family therapist, I talk to many parents whose experiences in a dysfunctional family of origin seem to prevent them from knowing how to express love to their own children in a meaningful, concrete way. Sometimes the stress and frustration they are encountering with a particular child or situation interferes with their ability to think creatively about new ways to express love. Many times the spiritual connection between the love God has for us and the love we are able to share with others seems to be missing.

My work with Christian families has blessed me in many ways, and I am pleased to have the opportunity to share these blessings through these easily accessible, practical suggestions. Writing this book has given me a chance to express my own faith and realize how it has had an impact on my parenting and my marital relationship.

My hope is that you will find this book both helpful and encouraging. It is meant to inspire, rather than to induce guilt. I have not been successful in implementing all the ideas shared within. As my husband and children will confirm, I am not a perfect wife and mother and never will be. Nevertheless, as a forgiven child of God I do rest secure in the grace of God, through Jesus Christ, which enables me to continue. On the most difficult days, His Holy Spirit provides courage and strength to go on. To Him be all the glory for any successes I have experienced as a mother or a wife. I am confident His love is meant for everyone and He can do for others what He has done for me.

1

PICTURE
A SPECIAL FUTURE

It was a warm autumn afternoon with a light breeze drifting through the screen door of our 80-year-old home. I was standing at the dining room table concentrating on a sewing project. My daughter knelt on a chair across from me, chin in hand, watching closely and peppering me with questions. With her older brother in school, she knew she had me all to herself and she was going to take advantage of it. Her blue eyes sparkled as she rattled on. There were lots of things she needed to know and "talk over." I was a little annoyed with her constant chattering, especially as I was trying to focus on the project in front of me. She caught me off guard when she looked up at me and said with a sigh, "Mom, when I grow up I want to be just like you. But it's going to be hard."

Oh, the insight of 4-year-olds! I was humbled. Was I the best role model for my child? I know my shortcomings all too well. Perhaps I should encourage her to model herself after someone else. I was worried. I didn't think she and I possessed all the same personality traits. Would she be discouraged if she couldn't be "just like me"? My daughter had just paid me a priceless compliment and I hardly knew how to respond. She was envisioning her own future at four years of age, and she already had some idea of how she wanted it to look.

I expect most parents have had a similar experience. Suddenly they realize what a significant person they are in their child's eyes, and they struggle with mixed feelings of pride and anxiety, contemplating the impact they are having on their child's future. They may reflect on the influence of their own parents and make a decision to do equally as well in rearing their offspring. Or they may remember some painful moments from their upbringing and resolve never to put their own child through the ridicule, comparison, or criticism they experienced.

Whatever the scenario, few would deny the importance of picturing a special future for one's child. That future is, of course, affected by our interaction with our children on a daily basis. What they see us model will have an important bearing on their personal habits and lifestyle well into adulthood. The same little girl who wanted to be just like me had stopped me short a few months earlier when she called from the back of the station wagon, "Mom, I'm the good one, aren't I? And Andrew is the bad one, isn't he?" Because neither child was doing anything particularly naughty at the moment, I knew her comment was not related to her brother's behavior but rather to her perception that *he* was always getting into trouble and *she* was not. I wondered what Andrew thought of himself. Was his picture of his future as bright as hers?

Uncomfortable with my own thoughts, I recalled how many times I had described in vivid detail for my friends the latest antics of my son. I had rolled my eyes and heaved a sigh wondering, "What on earth will we do with him?" Apparently my words and actions had not gone unnoticed by my daughter. What effect were they having on Andrew? I resolved then and there to speak more positively about my son. He is a gift from God with many talents and abilities. I needed to let him know that no one is good without Jesus, but because of Jesus' redeeming work on the cross, both he and his sister are perfect in the sight of God. And He has a special plan for both of their lives.

But what about being more intentional in shaping a vision for the future? How is it possible to capitalize on the developing strengths of a child, or the dreams of a spouse, and give them the confidence they need to develop the gifts God has given? The beginning of a new year is a good time to ask these questions. In January we often take a look back over what has been accomplished in the previous year. Similarly, we also look ahead at the clean calendar pages before us. We can take an active role now in helping each member of our family realize and express the areas of giftedness

God has given them. We can agree with Jeremiah as he spoke words of encouragement to the exiles in Babylon:

"For I know the plans I have for you," declares the LORD, *"plans to prosper you and not to harm you, plans to give you hope and a future. Then you will call upon Me and come and pray to Me, and I will listen to you. You will seek Me and find Me when you seek Me with all your heart." (Jeremiah 29:11–13)*

Take a look at the following ideas for shaping a positive, hope-filled future for your family. The ideas are divided into four categories, one for each week of the month. Challenge yourself to use at least one idea every seven days. See if God doesn't make a difference in your outlook and theirs.

Build Confidence

This first week focuses on building self-esteem. When we look into the future we look into the unknown. To overcome our fears and picture a future designed by God, we first acknowledge His overwhelming gift of sending His Son to the cross to win us forgiveness and eternal life. Our self-esteem doesn't come from what we have done but from what Christ has done for us. Secure in God's unconditional love, we thank Him for the gifts and abilities He has given us. We are valuable to God because we are His. He is applauding our efforts to grow and use the gifts He has given, just as a proud parent cheers on a Little League athlete or a first-year pianist. God couldn't be happier that we are stretching and growing, confident of His love.

Use some of the following ideas to share God's love with your husband and children. Let them know how valuable they are to you and to Him.

1. Use one of the following phrases at least once a day for the following week:

   ❏ I like the way you …

   ❏ I bet you feel good about the way you …

   ❏ You have a lot to offer. Thanks for sharing …

2. To get a glimpse of what your child or husband thinks of himself or herself, have each family member complete the following statements:

❏ People say I'm good at ...

❏ I think God made me good at ...

3. Ask each family member to describe personal strengths. Make a list of these strengths and talk about how they are gifts from God. Reflect on various individuals from the Bible to whom God gave special gifts to do His work. Consider Abraham, Moses, Samson, Hannah, Elizabeth, Mary, Paul, and so on.

4. Choose an encouraging Bible passage that emphasizes our value and worth to God. Read it aloud at bedtime or family devotion time, inserting each family member's name in the appropriate place(s). For example:

> God so loved [Andrew] that He gave His one and only Son that [Andrew who] believes in Him shall not perish but have eternal life. For God did not send His Son into the world to condemn [Andrew], but to save [Andrew] through Him. (John 3:16–17)

5. Plan a You-Are-Special Day for each member of the family. Each person will receive uplifting notes from other family members that express their appreciation and encouragement. Notes

might begin with, "I'm glad you're in our family because ... "

6. Write a family member's name on a large sheet of paper. Post the paper on the refrigerator door, a bulletin board, or some other public place. Encourage each family member to write positive comments or descriptive words about the "person of the week" in the blank space provided.

7. Build an encouragement acrostic using the letters of each family member's name. This might be done at a family meeting or as part of devotion time with all participants brainstorming ideas together. (Hint: Use a dictionary or thesaurus to help you, but keep the vocabulary appropriate for your children's level of understanding.) Display the results of your efforts in a prominent place. Following are two examples:

M erry	**A** nimated
I nteresting	**N** oteworthy
R adiant in Christ	**D** ramatic
I ntellectual	**R** edeemed by God
A greeable	**E** nergetic
M agnanimous	**W** insome

8. Pass on a positive remark you've heard someone else make about your husband or children. For instance:

Mrs. Anderson told me how helpful you

were after school today.

Mark mentioned that you made an excellent presentation at the meeting last week.

Mrs. Martin said how much she appreciated your help in the nursery last Sunday. She mentioned that you really seem to have a way with children.

9. Ask your children or husband about their plans, goals, or activities for the week ahead. Let them know you are praying for them to do their best. Volunteer to pray with them.

∽ Week 2 ∽

Dream

Part of picturing a special future for our loved ones is helping them to dream dreams. Ralph Waldo Emerson wrote, "Imagination expands and exalts us." If this is true, then we certainly need to work on creating an environment that will help our loved ones expand their horizons and lift their sights to the great things God has in store for them. The following ideas are designed to do just that.

1. At dinner one night this week, ask each family member to list three things they would like to be able to do

    ➤ in the next year.

    ➤ in the next three to five years.

    ➤ in the next ten years (or when they grow up).

2. At a family mealtime this week, ask each family member to name at least two things they would like to have the family do together in the coming year.

3. Ask each family member to finish this sentence:

    I don't know much about _____ , *but if I could, I'd like to learn more.*

4. Visit a museum as a family. Ask each individual

to tell which area they found most interesting and why.

5. If you have teenagers, give each member of the family a predetermined amount of money, e.g., $20. Ask them to spend the next six months increasing the "investment." Periodically check in on everyone's progress. This is a perfect opportunity to discuss good stewardship of our financial gifts from God. As a family, talk about budgeting, tithing, investment opportunities, and wise spending.

6. Visit the library and choose an age-appropriate book about a famous person who dared to dream and then worked hard to achieve the dream. Read the book together as a family. If reading is not possible, use a video about a famous person or listen to a book on tape in the car. Ask how God might have blessed that achievement and used it to help others.

7. Plan a vocational theme week. Allow each family member to select one vocational interest area they want to learn more about. Visit the library to get more information, or plan a family field trip to a place where this particular work is done. If possible, ask someone employed in this area to talk more with your family about his or her occupation.

8. Be sure your children understand and appreciate your husband's field of work as well as your own. If possible, plan a field trip and lunch with Dad or Mom at work.

Week 3

Discover Areas of Giftedness

Even adults sometimes have trouble knowing what they're good at doing. In 1 Corinthians 12, we are told that all Christians are given gifts for the common good. Use this week to help family members discover unique ways in which God has gifted them. Emphasize the importance of trying new things rather than succeeding at every undertaking. Our heavenly Father values the condition of our hearts more highly than our accomplishments.

1. At supper one night, ask each family member to complete this group of sentences:

    ➤ One thing God has made me good at is ...

    ➤ I could be even better if I ...

    ➤ The help I would like from each of you is ...

2. Encourage each family member to try one new experience in the next month. For example, if a youngster is normally sports minded, she might try an art, drama, or music experience.

3. For a smaller step, pursue other avenues related to a particular interest area. Someone focused on participating in athletics might expand this interest by reading a book about a sports figure; helping a younger child improve his skill; trying a new, non-competitive sport; or visiting a sports museum.

A smaller step made in the area of music might mean attending a concert featuring a different style of music than one normally listens to; learning about a composer, singer, or musician; using one's musical talent for others in a worship service or at a nursing home; or learning to play a different instrument.

4. With family input, plan one activity in each of the following categories to take place over the next three to four months.

> Reading

> Athletics

> Outdoor activities (hiking, nature, picnic, etc.)

> Music

> Drama

> Helping others

Some of these areas may be combined, such as attending a musical theater production or reading a book to someone who can't read for themselves. The goal is to examine new possibilities, expand horizons, and discover unrecognized gifts.

5. Study a foreign country as a family. Visit the public library for information. Read age-appropriate books together about people and places in that land. With the help of each family member, make a meal characteristic of this nation.

Find out how many Christians live in the country you are studying and what is being done to share Christ there. Talk about how each member of your family could use his or her abilities to show Christ's love to the people of this land, both now and in the future.

6. Ask each family member to complete the following phrases:

   ➤ I'd like to know more about …

   ➤ If I knew I wouldn't fail or be embarrassed, I'd like to try …

7. As a parent, be willing to join a child in a new undertaking. A mother and daughter might take cross-country skiing lessons together. A father and son might try their hand at baking a pie.

8. Take time this week to express an active interest in a child's or husband's hobby, even if it doesn't match your own interests. This might mean reading the sports page to learn something about basketball, even if you don't enjoy playing or watching the game.

∞ Week 4 ∞

Meet Challenges

By now the members of your family may have discovered several new interests they would like to explore or areas of giftedness they would like to strengthen. New challenges are exciting, but working on building skills requires discipline. We all experience some setbacks on the road to success. The following ideas are designed to help you help your children and husband "keep on" as they pursue their dreams and desires

1. Share an age-appropriate short story with family members about someone who overcame a difficulty to achieve a goal. This might be fictional (*The Little Engine That Could*) or a real-life account as found in *Reader's Digest* or a Christian magazine like *Guideposts*. Explain that just "trying hard" isn't the secret to success. God has won our ultimate victory for us, and He guides us through every earthly achievement.

2. At a family mealtime this week, ask each family member to complete these sentences:

   ➤ One thing I need to ask God to help me work on is …

   ➤ One small thing I could do this week to improve is …

3. Work on a jigsaw puzzle as a family. This activity underscores the fact that every individual plays a part in putting together a whole picture. It also provides an added dividend by encouraging family members to talk.

4. As family members set goals this month, encourage them by reminding them of God's promises. Write one of the following Scripture verses on a small note and tuck it into a lunch bag or briefcase, under a pillow, or inside a pocket.

> *I can do everything through Him who gives me strength. (Philippians 4:13)*

> *That is why, for Christ's sake, I delight in weaknesses, in insults, in hardships, in persecutions, in difficulties. For when I am weak, then I am strong. (2 Corinthians 12:10)*

> *Consider it pure joy, my brothers, whenever you face trials of many kinds, because you know that the testing of your faith develops perseverance. Perseverance must finish its work so that you may be mature and complete, not lacking anything. (James 1:2–4)*

5. Provide consistent positive feedback, especially when someone tries a new activity. Comments such as "I'm glad you were willing to try that!" and "I bet you're proud of yourself for attempting something new!" are especially helpful.

6. Visual reminders are an important encouragement. Purchase a small bag of stickers or stars, and use them to mark a calendar or chart for every day a family member accomplishes a goal or task she has set for herself.

7. Celebrate small victories. Light a special candle. Thank God for the blessings He gave you in your Baptism and the blessings He gives you today. Fly a family flag. Hang a banner. Use the good dishes. Plan a favorite meal.

2

Express Love
Through Touch

Squeals of laughter filled the house as our children begged, "Give me a total body hug, Daddy. Come on, do it right now! If I get in bed right now, can I be first? Please, Daddy, please!"

These sounds regularly filled our house at bedtime when our children were younger, and they taught me something important. There are days when kind words and gentle hugs from Mom are nice, but wrestling with Dad is best of all. Something about that "total body contact" says to a child, "You are all right. You are one of God's special creations, and you are also special to me."

Appropriate touching is an essential part of healthy development for boys and girls. In *Raising Good Children,* Dr. Thomas Lickona describes an American psychiatrist's study of 70 children reared in institutions for the first three years of their lives. Their physical needs were attended to, but the children received little social interaction or intellectual stimulation—in short, little touch or affection. These children were compared with 70 children in foster homes who generally received more attention and affection. The disturbing findings revealed that the institutionalized children seemed totally unable to control their impulses and showed an "incomprehensible cruelty to other children and animals." Dr. Lickona describes similar behavior in children raised in homes without love, which means homes without warmth, affection, and appropriate touch.

But physical contact is not just for kids. Adults need it too. At the death of a spouse, widows and widowers often report what they miss most is lack of human contact. According to James Lynch, author of *The Broken Heart*, adults who live alone die sooner from every kind of disease than do those who are married. One reason for this statistic, he believes, is that isolated people simply don't get touched often enough.

Residents of nursing homes have been known to improve mentally and emotionally when they are touched in a meaningful way. Researchers say appropriate, meaningful touch triggers physiological and biochemical changes that help protect the body against heart disease, cancer, infection, and stress-related illness. According to a study quoted in *McCalls* (November 1992), people who receive gentle, therapeutic touching experience a drop in blood pressure and an increase in oxygen-carrying hemoglobin in their blood. Even the body's levels of cortisol and adrenaline, both indicators of excess stress, drop in response to a daily half-hour massage. At times, animal contact can substitute for human contact when people lack attention and affection.

Unfortunately, lack of touch is not a problem reserved for old age or widowhood. Spouses frequently lose the habit of touching as the years pass. Kids come along and the pace of life speeds up. Psychologists describe ours as a low-contact culture compared to Latino, Mediterranean, and other high-contact cultures. In one study, psychologist Sidney Jourard observed people dining in various cafes around the world. He saw people touch one another 180 times per hour in San Juan, 110 times per hour in Paris, but only twice per hour in Gainesville, Florida, and not at all in London (*McCalls*, November 1992).

Given the importance of touch for health and well-being, any book on ways to love one's spouse and children would surely be remiss without considering this important element of love. In this month of hearts, flowers, and chocolate candy, it's important to consider how meaningful touch can open the door to a richer relationship with those we love.

Jesus certainly knew the value of touch for human beings. Remember how He related to little people.

> *Then they brought young children to Him, that He might touch them; but the disciples rebuked those who brought them. But when Jesus saw it, He was greatly displeased and said to them, "Let the little children come to Me, and do not forbid them; for of such is the kingdom of God." ... And He took them up in His arms, put His hands on them, and blessed them. (Mark 10:13–16 NKJV)*

It wasn't just the words that Jesus spoke, it was also His actions that said He loved and cared for these children. He made physical contact with them, picked them up, touched them, and spoke words of encouragement and value to them. His words and actions said, "You are important to Me."

Our Lord was aware of the importance of touch for people of all ages. The Bible tells us that Jesus not only spoke to many of the people He healed, He touched them as well. Consider the following:

> When [Jesus] came down from the mountainside, large crowds followed Him. A man with leprosy came and knelt before Him and said, "Lord, if You are willing, You can make me clean."
>
> Jesus reached out His hand and touched the man. ... Immediately he was cured of his leprosy. (Matthew 8:1–3; emphasis added)

> When [Jesus] had gone indoors, the blind men came to Him, and He asked them, "Do you believe that I am able to do this?"
>
> "Yes, Lord," they replied.
>
> Then He touched their eyes and said, "According to your faith will it be done to you"; and their sight was restored. (Matthew 9:28–30; emphasis added)

When the disciples heard this, they fell face-down to the ground, terrified. But Jesus came and touched them. "Get up," He said. "Don't be afraid." (Matthew 17:6–7; emphasis added)

Why did Jesus bother to touch these people when He could have reassured them with just His words? Perhaps it is because the embrace of a caring person imparts value to the recipient, regardless of age. We've already noted how Jesus cared for children and touched adults, but consider also the story of the prodigal son. Here a young man returns home after squandering his father's money on worthless living. In telling this story, Jesus describes the father's response, "But while he was still a long way off, his father saw him and was filled with compassion for him; he ran to his son, threw his arms around him and kissed him" (Luke 15:20).

The young man knew his father loved him, not only by his father's words but also by his actions. The loving embrace and warm kiss reassured him of his value emotionally as well as intellectually. Physical touch cemented the connection between his heart and his head.

Modern research confirms what God's Word already shows us. In *The Blessing,* Gary Smalley and John Trent describe an interesting study done by a neurosurgeon. With half of his hospital patients, the doctor sat on their bed and touched their arm or leg when he made his rounds. With his remaining patients, he stood near the bed to conduct his interview. Before the patients went home from the hospital, they were given a short questionnaire evaluating the treatment they had received. They were specifically asked to comment on the amount of time they felt the doctor had spent with them. Although the doctor had spent the same amount of time in each patient's room, the people whom he touched felt he had been in their room nearly twice as long as those he had not touched!

Touching is important. It imparts value, acknowledges acceptance, and expresses affection. But sometimes, appropriate touching is difficult to do. For those reared in homes where physical affection was rarely given, hugging and touching other family members may not come naturally. These parents and spouses have to consciously work at showing affection and sometimes wonder about what is "right."

Those raised in abusive homes, where touch was either violent or sexually inappropriate, may also have difficulty expressing warmth and intimacy through touch. Under these circumstances, counseling may help the adult wounded by improper touch to deal with the hurts of the past and form healthy patterns of affection in their present family relationships. The specific ideas that follow should also help adults learn how to express appropriate affection.

Finally, certain age groups often bring particular challenges. Late-elementary-school-aged boys and adolescents of both sexes may pose a problem for the parent who wants to continue expressing appropriate physical affection. The young people's developing independence causes them to resist contact. Touch at these times is still important, but it needs to be thoughtfully done. A child should not be made to feel uncomfortable because of touch, so special sensitivity may be needed to determine what feels comfortable (a pat on the back or a squeeze on the shoulder) and what does not (a good-night kiss or a good-bye hug). Every child is different and allowances for personal preference will often need to be made within the same family.

The next several pages offer suggestions for increasing physical contact with your children and spouse. Consider incorporating those you feel comfortable with into your everyday routine.

∽ Week 1 ∞

1. Hold hands while saying the blessing at the dinner table this evening.

2. Wake up each family member with a kiss on the forehead and a squeeze on the arm or shoulder.

3. Give each family member a hug and/or kiss before they leave for school or work.

4. Hold your child on your lap while reading him a story.

5. Have your child sit next to you, with your body touching hers, while you read a story, listen to music, or talk together.

6. Give your teenager or older child a pat on the back or squeeze on the shoulder as he passes you in the house.

7. For as long as your children enjoy it, hold their hands when walking or shopping. Parents sometimes give up this reassuring practice before a child is ready to let it go. Enjoy the contact while it lasts.

⌇∞⌇ Week 2 ⌇∞⌇

Flowers and gifts on Valentine's Day and birthdays are helpful in keeping romantic fires burning, but meaningful touch can stoke the fires of love all year round. Consider some of the following possibilities for your husband this coming week. Regular implementation could make a difference for years to come.

1. Husbands and wives often get so busy with work, parenting, and household tasks that they forget to take the time to touch each other. As a reminder this week, set the kitchen timer (or your watch) to go off every hour. When you are home together. When the timer goes off, find your husband and give him a hug or a kiss. He'll probably be surprised and pleased you thought of him so often.

2. Sit next to your husband in the car, shoulder to shoulder, as you did when you were dating—and don't forget to buckle that middle seat belt!

3. Snuggle up next to your mate on the sofa while watching a television program he enjoys.

4. Go to bed at the same time so you have an opportunity to lay next to each other, holding each other, before you fall asleep.

5. Hold hands as you go for a walk, as you watch a movie, or in church—wherever it would be comfortable and appropriate.

6. Tell your husband what you like about the way he makes love to you. Reinforce the positive things in your sexual relationship by expressing appreciation.

7. Ask your husband what he would like from you in your sexual relationship, for example, what kind of touch he most appreciates. Let him know you care about his wishes.

∞ Week 3 ∞

Touch is important as a part of our daily routine, but it can also be very comforting in times of stress. This week watch for ways to use physical touch in caring ways when family members are fatigued, discouraged, or stressed.

1. Offer a back rub, shoulder rub, or neck massage to a family member with a headache or tense muscles.

2. Lie in bed next to a little one who is frightened by a sudden storm or a scary nightmare until she is able to relax and fall back asleep. (This is better done in the child's bed rather than yours.)

3. Hold the hand of a family member encountering something frightening—such as a medical procedure, a big dog, or a new person. This small act can be very reassuring.

4. Put your arm around a family member who is feeling sad or lonely. This may mean putting your chair next to his or sitting on the bed next to him.

5. Hold a child who is worried or upset. Give her a feeling of safety with your arms wrapped around her.

6. As you pray with your child when he is upset, hold his hands in your own if he will allow it. If he resists this, try placing a hand on his knee or

shoulder while you pray with him.

7. Hold your husband's hand, or touch his arm, as you pray together about a particular concern. The nearness of another human being helps us feel less lonely when we are worried or afraid.

⌢ Week 4 ⌢

Touching can be done with more than the arms or hands. Touching can also be done with the eyes. When we make eye contact with people, we let them know they have our attention, that we are concentrating on what they say and do.

1. The next time your child begins to tell you a story about something she experienced, a movie she saw, or a book she read, put down what you are doing and look at her. Maintain comfortable eye contact with her all the way through her story.

2. Let your husband and children know you see them by commenting positively on their appearance. Try doing this at least once a day for the coming week.

3. If your husband or children begin to tell you something when you can't give them your full attention, tell them you'd really like to hear what they have to say when you can be more attentive. Don't forget to follow through on your promise as soon as possible.

4. Smile at your loved ones. Let them see through the sparkle in your eyes and the lift of your lips that you love and value them for no reason at all, except that they're yours. (This could also make them wonder what you're up to and add some

humor and mystery to your day.)

5. Play peekaboo with a young child. This will remind you again of how appealing eye contact is, even to the very young.

6. While we don't establish eye contact with God, it is important to remember that He sees us. His eyes are continually on us, wherever we are and whatever we do. Read the following Bible passage to a family member today as a reminder of our Lord's constant presence with us.

   From heaven the Lord looks down and sees all mankind; from His dwelling place He watches all who live on earth—He forms the hearts of all, who considers everything they do. (Psalm 33:13–15)

7. Eye contact is a two-way street. We can look at someone on our own, but contact is established only when the individual looks back. Knowing that God is looking at us is a great comfort and encouragement, but we are also encouraged to "look back." Hebrews 12:2 exhorts us to "fix our eyes on Jesus, the author and perfecter of our faith, who for the joy set before Him endured the cross, scorning its shame, and sat down at the right hand of the throne of God."

   At a family meal this week, talk about what it means to "fix our eyes on Jesus."

3

Prayer That
Touches
the Heart

It had been an uneventful evening. We'd watched
TV together before our familiar bedtime routine. Paja-
mas were donned. Teeth were brushed. That last glass
of water was drunk, and routine prayers were said
before the lights went out. Neither child seemed particularly worried or upset about any event of the day.
That's why I was surprised to hear my son still rustling
about more than a half hour after we'd turned out the
lights. I wondered what was up and suspected mis-
chief.

"What's wrong, Andrew? Why aren't you asleep?"
I asked.

"Mom."

"Yes."

"I want a dog."

Now I knew. We'd just received a letter from his
grandparents wondering what we planned to do with

our large dog, Jack, whom we'd left with them when we moved to our new home. Jack was not the kind of dog to enjoy tightly confined spaces and rental property. Evidently Andrew was missing Jack. "I wish we had a dog," he said again. "But I just don't know what to do about it."

In a moment of inspiration only God could give, I asked, "Would you like to pray about it?"

"Yes," he replied, "but you pray." And so we did. I told God how Andrew missed his friend Jack and how he wanted a dog. Then I hugged him tight, gave him a kiss, and tucked him in again. He seemed satisfied, but I wondered what God would do about the dog.

The next morning Andrew seemed a little clearer about the kind of dog he wanted. At breakfast he informed me, "Mom, I've been thinking. I want a dog like Aunt Mary and Uncle Phil have. That would be a good house dog."

"I know, honey, but miniature poodles—the kind of dog they have—cost lots of money," I patiently explained. "We don't have enough money now to buy a dog like that."

"I know," he insisted, "but I'd still like a little, white house dog like they have."

"We'll just have to wait and see," I responded without too much conviction. I wanted Andrew to face the prospect of no dog at all. We'd prayed, but I wasn't sure God would answer this prayer in the way my son hoped.

But God had a surprise for me! Later the same day,

as we went through the mail, Andrew and I spied an ad in the 4-H newsletter proclaiming: "Free to a good home: small, white dog—poodle/terrier mix. Dog has shots and has been spayed. Owner must agree to take 4-H dog-care classes." Although my husband was less than enthusiastic, we phoned immediately and discovered we were the first to contact the owners. With our children jumping up and down, we arranged a meeting for the coming Saturday. "This is just to see if we like her," we cautioned. But the kids had other ideas.

When we first laid our eyes on Nikki, it was love at first sight. It was clear the owners hated to let her go, but they were older and wanted to travel. They wanted to make sure she would go to a good home. There had been other callers after us, they said, but since we were the first to contact them, we could have the dog if we still wanted her.

Did we want her? Looking at my children, there was little doubt in my mind. Even though my husband had doubts about who would feed and water her, it was clear this little pooch was already pawing her way into the heart of every family member—especially my son. We took her home that day, and as if she knew who had prayed hardest for her, she slept on Andrew's bed that night. They continued to have a very special relationship for years to come.

Why do I share this anecdote? Because this small story of answered prayer helped to set the tone for prayer in our household. It reminded me again of something I'd read by Larry Christenson in *The Christian Family* years earlier.

If only we believed the Bible, and realized how unreservedly the child believes what he sings! There is not the slightest thought in his heart but that Jesus indeed does love him. His problem is not a lack of faith, but a lack of experience. The job of the parent is to let that faith become a doorway to experience. In concrete and practical ways the parents must help the child to recognize the love of Jesus in everyday affairs of life.

Now as I look back, how grateful I am for the prompting of the Holy Spirit at that moment when we prayed in Andrew's room. How thankful I am that God used me to help my child see how much his heavenly Father loves him. Our little white dog has been a daily reminder for years of God's love for His children. God hears their prayers and He answers.

But what about the prayers God doesn't answer in the ways we want? Surprisingly, our children never seemed to struggle with this as much as we did. We learned to pray about many things, some of which turned out quite differently than we imagined. Christenson points out that prayers answered differently than we expect are "a spur to further research." God always answers prayer in the way He knows is best for us. Surprising answers send us searching in His Word, asking His Spirit to guide us in the way God is leading.

For a Christian wife and mother, home maintenance most certainly involves prayer. Loving my children and my husband means lifting them up before God on a daily basis, petitioning Him on their behalf. It also means praying with them. I put my arms around them and talk to God with them. I sit on the edge of their beds at night as we address our heavenly Father. I share their secret fears and longings as we go to God together. I teach my children to pray and am my husband's most faithful prayer partner.

The problem with daily, intentional prayer is often one of time. There are so many things screaming for our attention that it's easy to leave this powerful home-maintenance tool on the shelf until damage has been done and some area of our family life is badly in need of repair. How can we make prayer a regular part of our family's care in today's busy world? Consider some of the following ideas for building your family's prayer life. Pick one or two you like and get started today.

⌒ Week 1 ⌒

One of the simplest forms of prayer is that of praise and thanksgiving. Most parents insist at a very young age that their children say thank you to someone who has given them a gift, yet they neglect teaching the same children to say thank You to their heavenly Father on a regular basis. This week's suggestions are designed to expand your family's awareness of God's goodness and grace and help you praise Him for these gifts on a regular basis. Use these ideas before or after family mealtimes, during family devotions, while riding in the car together, at bedtime, or whenever the occasion arises to praise God as a family.

1. Ask everyone to think of one thing for which to thank God. Go around the table or circle allowing each person to finish this sentence prayer: "Thank You, God, for ..."

2. To expand on the thank-You prayer and remind each other that everything we have is a gift from God, ask family members to thank God alphabetically, for example, "I thank God for *apples*." "I thank God for *bicycles*." "I thank God for *cats*." Continue all the way through the alphabet.

3. Help your family learn to praise God for who He is. With younger children, it is helpful to first talk about a friend or family member whom they like. For instance, you might ask, "What do you like about Grandma? What is the best thing about

her?" As the children identify Grandma's smile, the way she listens to them, the ways she gives them special things, and so on, you can also point out that there are special things about God that we enjoy as well. Though we cannot see God in the same way we see Grandma, Jesus helps us understand who God is and what He is like.

Read the account of Jesus blessing the children (Mark 10:13–16). Then ask, "If Jesus were sitting with us here today, what do you think you would like most about Him? What would He be like if He visited our family?" When everyone has identified something they like about Jesus, invite the family to join in a sentence prayer: "Dear Jesus, I like the way You ..."

4. As a follow-up to number 3, suggest that family members write a note or make a card that expresses their appreciation or affection for the special person they identified. Include a sentence or two that tells the person how he or she shows God's love to others. For example,

Dear Mrs. Jones,
Thank you for helping me when I scraped my
knee at school the other day. You reminded me
of how much God loves and cares for me.

Family members might then join in making a group card to God, thanking Him for who He is.

This could be posted on the refrigerator or family bulletin board as a reminder of God's love.

5. Sing a song of praise as a family. Depending on the ages of family members, musical talent, and preference, this could cover a wide variety of possibilities including singing a cappella, playing musical instruments, using a hymnal, singing along with an audiocassette of children's praise music, or lip-syncing with a contemporary Christian singer. Let the musical experience of praise be as varied and individual as each family member. The important thing is to help family members enjoy praising God.

6. Pray the psalms. Ask family members to alternate reading the verses of a selected psalm. You might try Psalms 92, 96, 98, 103, or 145–150.

7. Illustrate your praise to God by encouraging family members to make a collage or draw a picture of things for which they are thankful. Use these visual reminders as a means of increasing your family's "attitude of gratitude."

∽ Week 2 ∽

If we're honest, most of us would admit that the first thing that comes to mind when praying is to ask for something. It's relatively easy to teach children to ask God for something for themselves. It is more difficult to remind them, and ourselves, of the need to pray for others. In this second week of learning to use the tool of prayer, the focus is to ask God's Holy Spirit to hone our skills in praying for others.

1. Identify family members, including extended family, for whom to pray. Bring each family member's need to God and ask that the relative be especially assured of God's peace, protection, and love.

2. As a follow-up to number 1, send a postcard to every relative for whom you have prayed. You don't need to write a long message. Just say, "We love you. We're thinking of you. We prayed for you today." You might invite relatives to give you specific prayer concerns.

3. Use Christmas cards as prayer reminders. Beginning in January, choose one card a day and pray for the sender. Call or send a note to tell your loved ones they are in your thoughts and prayers.

4. Using the Sunday bulletin as a guide, pray for your church and its leaders. Beginning with the

pastor and any additional staff members, pray for each one and his or her family by name. Include leaders of various boards, projects, and committees, as well as Sunday school teachers. Ask God to strengthen and guide your church staff members in the work they are doing.

5. Join together in praying for your child's school, its administrators, its teachers, and its secretaries and support staff. This is also a good time to ask your child for names of classmates for whom she would like to pray.

6. Pray for your community. Along with teaching your child about local government, this prayer exercise reminds us that God intends for us to be "salt" and "light" in a dark world.

7. Using a newspaper or information from the evening news, pray for people and concerns beyond your own community. Pray for the president and other government officials. Those in war-torn countries or those suffering from natural disasters might also be included.

∽ Week 3 ∽

Sometimes we are tempted to avoid the confessional aspect of prayer. Confession requires that we be honest with God, with our families, and with ourselves. Through confession, we take a good look at ourselves and see how often we have fallen short of what God wants us to do. We admit our weaknesses and shortcomings. We recognize that we are sinners.

Don't be tempted to overlook this part of prayer life and leave it to a formalized ritual on Sunday morning. God calls us, for the sake of His Son, to come quickly to Him when we sin. He longs for us to bring our brokenness to Him because only He has the power to make us new again.

The ideas that follow are intended to help you and your family expand the confessional part of your prayer life. Unlike ideas presented in previous sections, they are presented sequentially, that is, each idea is intended to build on the one previous to it. Starting small and building toward a greater depth of honesty will help family members be open with one another. Confession brings us peace and great joy—joy in knowing that when we confess our failures, God is faithful to forgive us and restore our relationship with Him. Learn to celebrate God's forgiveness as a family.

1. Read Exodus 20:1–21 as a family. (If your children are young, read this portion of Scripture from a children's Bible or paraphrase the passage in your own words.) Talk about the Ten Com-

mandments. Why did God give these laws to His people? How did God's people fail to keep the Ten Commandments perfectly as He wanted them to do? How do we fail to keep the Ten Commandments? Don't embarrass your children or make them feel threatened as you talk about failure to keep God's commands. Share faults of your own and express your thankfulness for God's forgiveness.

As a family, use words like these as you pray:

> *Dear God, we know that You want us to reflect Your love to others by the way we live and by the way we treat each other. Many times we fail to do this. Forgive us, Lord, for Jesus' sake. Through your Holy Spirit, make us more like You each day. Amen.*

2. Read Exodus 20:3–6. Discuss these verses with your family. What does it mean to have "other gods"? What are some other gods we have today? Explain that material possessions and pleasures can become gods if we place them first in our thoughts, before our heavenly Father. Set the tone for confession by telling about a time when you "worshiped other gods" before you worshiped the Lord.

   When you're sure everyone understands the concept of worshiping other gods, hand out pieces of paper and ask each person to write down or draw a picture of a god each is tempted to worship. When everyone has finished, you might pray together:

Dear Lord, we confess we often fail to keep You first in our hearts and lives. We put many other things before You. Forgive us, Lord, for Jesus' sake. Following You is the most important thing we want to do. In Jesus' name. Amen.

After praying, collect the pieces of paper and burn them or tear them to shreds. Explain that when God forgives our sins, they are gone. We begin again with a clean slate. Model placing God first for your family. Pray before meals. Make time for reading His Word. Plan weekend schedules around worship. Explain how you set aside your church offering before paying bills.

3. Read Exodus 20:7–8. Discuss these commands with your family. How do we sometimes misuse God's name? How could we forget to keep the Sabbath day holy? Again distribute small slips of paper and ask each family member to write or draw a picture of a way he or she has failed to honor God by misusing His name or day. Use words like these to confess your sins:

Dear Lord, we confess we don't honor Your name as we should. We misuse it in anger. We treat it disrespectfully in front of

*others. We often dishonor Your day of wor-
ship. Our minds are on other things. We are
grumpy and cross. We forget that this one
day is set aside to honor You. Forgive us,
Lord, for Jesus' sake. Through Your Holy
Spirit, give us great joy in living for You,
honoring Your name with our lives, and worshiping You. Amen.*

Once again destroy the papers as a visual
reminder of how God forgives our sins. Then
plan some activities to honor God's name. Design
and display a family banner praising Him. Ask
family members to list their favorite names for
God—Shepherd, Light of the world, Father.
Brainstorm the many ways you honor God's
name—praying and singing, sharing your faith,
reading His Word. Plan a special Sunday celebration—church, time spent outdoors to thank Him
for His creation, etc.

4. Read Exodus 20:12–13. Ask family members to
tell about some ways you can "honor your father
and your mother." Describe ways you honor
your own parents. Discuss how we can murder
someone without actually taking a physical life.
(See 1 John 3:15.) Ask family members to complete the following sentences:

➤ I honor my father or mother when I ...

➤ I treat someone with love and respect when I ...

Confess times when you have failed to honor one another. Use the words "I'm sorry" and "I forgive you" often in your home.

5. Read Exodus 20:14–15. You may want to read the appropriate books from the series Learning about Sex (Concordia, 1995) with your children. Teach them that their sexuality is a gift from God. Talk together about inappropriate messages aimed at children and teens in the media.

   Celebrate your sexuality and your husband's as gifts from God. Leave a love note on the bathroom mirror or in his briefcase. Recreate one of your early dates. Plan time to be alone together. Take him to a romantic restaurant for dinner and spend the meal holding his hand and looking deeply into his eyes. Body and eye contact is as important as verbal or written messages.

   Model for your children how to respect property and take care of their possessions, as well as treat their siblings' and friends' things properly.

6. Read Exodus 20:16–17. Ask you family how we "give false testimony" against our neighbor. Confess times in your own life when you have gossiped or put people down. Let your children hear you telling your husband and others about their accomplishments and good behaviors. Do the same for your husband—commenting on his spe-

cial qualities to your children and friends!

Discuss the word *covet*. As a family, brainstorm the many blessings you enjoy. Model for your children contentment with the blessings God has given. Confess times when you have said hurtful things and coveted others' belongings. Remind each family member that as God's children, we can pronounce God's forgiveness to each other. Confessions can be handled simply by saying to the confessor, "God forgives you and so do I."

Week 4

Though we have spent much of the month praising God, praying for others, and confessing our sins, it is also very fitting for us to regularly approach God for our own personal needs. God wants and reminds us to come to Him with all our cares and concerns. This last section highlights ways we can let our personal needs be known as we pray for each other in a family setting.

1. Using "Cast all your anxiety on Him because He cares for you" (1 Peter 5:7) as a reference point, ask each family member how they would like you to pray for them this week. Let them know that all their concerns are important to you and to God.

2. Share one or more of your own prayer requests with family members. Let them know their prayers for you are equally effective and important to God.

3. Start a family prayer journal. Record family prayer requests in it, along with God's answers.

4. Make a family prayer board. Family members can post prayer concerns using self-stick notes or paper and thumbtacks. In busy families, this can be especially useful for helping family members keep in touch with each other.

5. Take time to pray with each other. This may happen at bedtime, mealtime, or anytime two family members are together in a quiet spot. Short sentence prayers can be especially useful at busy

moments and emphasize to our children that prayers needn't be long and formal to be effective.

6. Try a round-robin prayer with your husband. One partner begins the prayer. The other partner responds with his or her own prayer about the same topic. The original partner introduces another subject with a short prayer and the second partner responds with another short prayer of his or her own. In this way the prayer continues circulating between the two partners until all topics are covered. For example:

> *Todd:* Dear Lord, please be with Jeremy today and help him do his best on his arithmetic test.

> *Sue:* Yes, Lord, we ask that You would help him think clearly and check his work carefully.

> *Todd:* We also ask for your guidance in Danielle's life as she tries to decide on which college to attend.

> *Sue:* We ask that her decision would honor You, Lord.

7. If extemporaneous prayer feels difficult or uncomfortable, ask your husband to read prepared prayers with you. Prayer books, hymnals, and devotional books are good sources of prayers. You might also choose to use one of the psalms, reading alternating verses as a couple.

4

EXPRESS LOVE
WITH BOUNDARIES
AND STANDARDS

She looked worried, a little frightened, and tired. Her husband did not know she had come, but she said she had to talk to someone. Their marriage wasn't going well, and she didn't know what to do. She wondered if I could help.

When I asked about the problem, she related incident after incident in which her husband had verbally abused her. Even though she had a college degree and held a responsible managerial position, he said she was stupid and "no kind of mother." He berated her for not having meals when he wanted them, for not having the house as clean as he thought it ought to be, and for not being able to get him up on time in the morning. "Any kind of wife," he said, "would be able to do these things."

"Is there something else I can do?" she asked.

Sadly, I shook my head. I knew what this woman

needed to do. She needed to take *less* responsibility for her husband's happiness, not more. Only in establishing some important boundaries around herself, allowing him to be responsible for his own actions, could she truly love him in a way he needed to be loved.

Years earlier, when this woman's husband had been a little boy, his mother failed to love him in a way that encouraged responsibility and self-control. When he refused to get out of bed for school in the morning, she begged and pleaded with him to get up so he wouldn't be late. When he dawdled during breakfast, she threatened to let him go to school hungry, but she never followed through on her threat. She made herself responsible for most of his mistakes, so when he blamed her for not driving fast enough after he missed the school bus, she just clenched her teeth and tried to concentrate on driving faster. When he forgot his lunch at home and refused to eat the cafeteria food, she made sure she dropped off his lunch at school by noon. Whenever he got in trouble at school, she never failed to call the teacher and principal to let them know how unfairly her boy was being treated. When he verbally berated her for being so dumb, she passed it off as "just a phase" and continued trying to make him happy. In short, she made it her responsibility to make her son as happy and as satisfied with life as possible.

Now, more than a decade later, this little boy had grown into a man who was treating his wife in much the same way he had treated his mother. If he was two hours late for supper, she was blamed for not having a hot dinner waiting for him. If he was late for work, it was her fault for not getting him up on time—even though she'd tried valiantly for more than an hour to get him out of bed. He blamed her for all of his unhappiness, calling her stupid and lazy. Even though he was unable to keep a steady job, he regularly criticized her for the hours she spent at work. She kept trying to please him but only felt more miserable and resentful inside. "Is this really what love is all about?" she asked.

Contrast this situation with others I have known. Joshua, for instance, came from a home where his parents loved him but also knew he must learn to be responsible for himself. Their nightly routine called for Joshua to put his book bag by the door when he finished his homework so it would be ready to go the next morning. Sometimes Joshua did this; sometimes he forgot—even though he received at least one reminder.

The day came when Joshua realized, as he got out of the car at school, that he did not have his book bag. His mother had rescued him on previous occasions, but this morning she firmly shook her head and said he would have to do without it for the day. He wasn't happy about facing his teacher without his homework, but he learned something important about being responsible. It was a lesson possibly more beneficial than anything his math book might have taught him.

Or consider Chelsea. Her mother routinely did the family laundry on Friday mornings. She asked her children to have their dirty clothes in the laundry baskets in front of the washer and dryer before they went to school. Sometimes Chelsea remembered to do this, but often she forgot. Chelsea's mother frequently scolded her about not helping out and repeatedly reminded her on Fridays to get her laundry ready before she went to school, but nothing much seemed to help.

Finally, Chelsea's mother decided to have a talk with her daughter. She told Chelsea she would no longer nag her to get her clothes ready for washing on Friday. In fact, she said, Chelsea would not have to have laundry ready on any set day at all. From now on, Chelsea was free to do her own laundry. Chelsea's mother said she would be happy to help her daughter get started with running the washer and dryer, but the ultimate responsibility was her daughter's.

Initially, Chelsea wasn't perturbed by her mother's change in routine. Knowing her mother, Chelsea felt certain the new regimen would not last. Eventually, though, reality began to sink in. Monday morning came, and Chelsea had no clean jeans to wear to school. She began to realize she would have to wear a dirty pair or wash something quickly and go to school wearing damp clothing. She chose the latter, and she began to learn an important lesson in caring for herself and in respecting her mother's boundaries.

And then there was Brian. He hated to go to bed at night. When he was supposed to be asleep, he was often under his bed covers reading a book or playing a game. Consequently, Brian was also very difficult to get out of bed in the morning. He slowed down everyone in the family and made his sister miserable as his slow pace threatened to make them late nearly every day. Though his mother scolded and threatened, Brian continued to move with the speed of a box turtle, seemingly oblivious to the chaos around him.

Finally Brian's mother decided she had truly had enough. One day, as Brian dawdled along and the clock ticked on, Brian's mother got his sister in the car and drove off to school without him. He was 10 years old, old enough to leave alone for a short time, but his mother's behavior caught him completely off guard. His tearful, screaming, beet-red face in the rearview mirror was enough to tear at any mother's heart, but Brian's mother was determined. She kept driving.

It was a much more compliant Brian who answered his mother's phone call 15 minutes later. She confirmed that she would be back to get him, but it would be a half hour or so. He would just have to explain to the teacher why he was late. Gently, but firmly, she ended the phone call and gave Brian a little more time to think. As promised she showed up half an hour later and took Brian to school, leaving him to explain his tardiness to the teacher. It was some time before Brian decided to delay getting ready for school again.

———

Perhaps one of the most misused tools in the home-maintenance toolbox is that of discipline. Either we use it too little, creating a permissive environment with shaky rules and standards, or we use it too harshly, creating a rigid, inflexible setting where the authority of the parent is never questioned. Finding a middle ground is tricky, requiring one to blend equal amounts of support and control.

Much of this book is devoted to a supportive kind of love, that is, the kind of love that lets family members know they are valued. It requires intentional involvement with husband and children, a commitment of time and energy, letting them know they matter.

For many it's easy to see the connection of time and attention when it comes to building relationships. But it's much more challenging to connect the same factors to the harder side of love—the side that sets standards, monitors behavior, and enforces consequences. This is the side of love that teaches self-discipline, models respect, and allows the consequences of one's actions to do the teaching. It means allowing momentary unhappiness and unpleasantness to occur so that long-term goals can be accomplished. It's not an easy side of love to share, but it is a very necessary one.

Jesus gives us a perfect example of this firm aspect of love in His encounter with a rich young man. In Mark 10:17, the young man asks Jesus, "Good teacher, what must I do to inherit eternal life?"

Jesus responds by asking if the man knows the commandments, and he replies, "All these I have kept since I was a boy" (10:20).

At this point something very interesting happens. Mark's account tells us, "Jesus looked at him and *loved him*" (emphasis added). Jesus then responded with some very hard words for the man to hear. He said,

"One thing you lack. Go, sell everything you have and give to the poor, and you will have treasure in heaven. Then come, follow Me" (10:21).

The softer, more nurturing moms among us might have gasped in disapproval if Jesus had said this to our children. After all, didn't Jesus realize how much the young man wanted His approval? What about keeping things on a more positive note and recognizing the young man's efforts? We might be tempted to view Jesus as harsh and unyielding, but we must not forget what Mark recorded very clearly: "Jesus looked at him and *loved him*."

Jesus did not verbally challenge and correct this man with resentment, anger, or frustration. Rather, He loved him. He knew the man's greatest need, at this point, was to see what separated him from the kingdom of heaven. It hurt the man to learn he was not "good enough" and never would be. It hurt the man to find he needed to be separated from what was most important in his life. Out of love, Jesus chose to "hurt" him for a little while, so that the rich young man might have greater joy later on.

This chapter is devoted to the harder side of love, but one just as essential if a child is to mature into a healthy adult. It emphasizes boundaries that establish order and give feelings of safety and security. This side of love keeps the necessary balance in a marital relationship so that self-respect can flourish. Consider the following ideas as starters for loving your family in a new way or as reinforcement for the sturdy kind of love you've already got going.

∞ Week 1 ∞

1. As a family, talk about boundaries and limits. Ask each person to explain why rules and limits are important. Use some of the following questions as discussion starters: What do you think would happen if there were no speed limits? Why do farmers have fences around their livestock? Why do we have boundary lines between people's property? What would happen if there were no boundary lines?

2. As a family, talk about boundaries within the family. Ask what the word *private* means. Why is it important for family members to have privacy?

3. Ask each family member to talk about what he or she considers to be private or personal. All may agree that personal letters and time in the bathroom should be private, but some members may have difficulty concurring on other areas of personal space, especially if two children share a bedroom. Talk about ways each family member can have personal space and time alone.

4. Talk about rules and standards for maintaining personal privacy. This may mean allotting each child so much time in the bathroom without being hassled or marking certain items off limits to others unless the owner gives permission.

5. As a family, establish consequences for violating

the privacy rules. For instance, if Erica's brother reads her personal mail without her permission, it is agreed he will do her chores for a week.

6. Ask your husband if there are any ways in which he feels you are invading his privacy or personal space. For instance, he may be unhappy with the way you rearrange his desk, complain about his workroom, or go through his mail. Take time to clear the air on this topic.

7. Share with your husband your own needs for privacy. Communicating your personal needs hclps to avoid misundcrstandings and hurt feelings.

∞ Week 2 ∞

Boundaries are more than visible borders. They also include rules and standards to protect us. Deuteronomy contains a strong directive for parents to teach their children God's ways and help them obey His commands. Here Moses speaks to the children of Israel saying:

> *Love the LORD your God with all your heart and with all your soul and with all your strength. These commandments that I give you today are to be upon your hearts. Impress them on your children. Talk about them when you sit at home and when you walk along the road, when you lie down and when you get up. Tie them as symbols on your hands and bind them on your foreheads. Write them on the doorframes of your houses and on your gates. (Deuteronomy 6:5–9)*

This week's suggestions are intended to help family members grow in the ways they love, honor, and respect God. Some ideas may already be second nature to your family, but consciously drawing attention to them as ways we show honor and respect can help everyone grow in this area.

1. Attend a weekend worship service and resist the temptation to criticize any portion of the service.

2. Discuss the Third Commandment, "Remember the Sabbath day by keeping it holy" (Exodus

20:8). Ask for some suggestions on how to make Sunday a special day for honoring the Lord. Answers might include the following:

> We can go to bed earlier on Saturday night so we will be ready and rested to worship the Lord.

> We can have a breakfast treat on Sunday morning because it is a special day.

> We can play Christian music at home and in the car on Sunday morning to remind us whose day it is.

3. Set an extra place at the dinner table for Jesus, our unseen guest. Ask family members how their behavior would be different if they were more conscious of Jesus' presence. Ask for some suggestions on how to honor God at mealtimes.

4. Talk about the custom of wearing good clothes for worship services. Where did we get this practice of dressing up? What do you think of dressing up for worship? How does it honor God?

5. Read the parable of the Pharisee and the tax collector in Luke 18:9–14. Discuss the parable. How did each man honor or dishonor God? How can people appear to be honoring God, while not honoring Him in their hearts? (As a parent, describe a time when this happened to you so family members will be more willing to be honest with themselves.)

6. We honor God in the way we talk to Him. Brainstorm some Bible names for God that honor Him, for example, Wonderful Counselor, Savior, Creator, and Bread of life. Use them in your prayers this week.

7. Review the first three commandments and talk together about how they are intended to be boundaries for our relationship with God.

⚭ Week 3 ⚭

God calls parents and children to reflect their love for Him as they live together in harmony. There is to be something different about Christian families and the way they relate to one another—something that testifies to others about the God they serve. This week's ideas are intended to help family members consciously consider how to love and respect each other in practical ways.

1. Use only respectful names to address each other. Insist that your children address you respectfully, and be careful to treat them in the same manner. Ask each family member how they prefer to be addressed. Avoid using names with which they may be uncomfortable or embarrassed.

2. Insist that children address each other respectfully. As a family, talk about consequences for name calling. For example, one found guilty of teasing or taunting another family member will put a quarter in the family bank. This money can then be donated to a charity or a mission project.

3. Learn and practice mealtime manners. Clearly explain expectations and benefits of courteous behavior. Make a game of catching offenders so that reminders can be given in a positive fashion. For example, anyone who belches at the table must go to their room and count loudly to 100. Or anyone who eats before the mealtime prayer

must run around the exterior of the house three times before eating another bite of the meal.

4. Learn and practice phone etiquette. Encourage children to answer the phone politely, for example, "Hello, this is the Martin house. May I help you?" Practice being courteous while someone else is on the phone and taking phone messages for another member of the family. Assist your family in deciding on standards of behavior for phone usage as well as consequences for rule infractions.

   This also would be an excellent time to review phone safety. Make sure young children know how to answer the phone and take messages if they're home alone. Some criminals prey on children who answer the phone and indicate adults are not present. Make sure emergency numbers are posted in easy-to-find places and that even your youngest child knows how to dial 911.

5. Discuss how family members will use shared space such as the family room. Who will be responsible for picking up toys? Who will put the pillows back on the couch? Who will pick up the newspapers? Talk about the importance of showing respect for each other by sharing responsibility for group areas in the home.

6. Talk about how family members will treat shared

objects in the home such as the television, a computer, the car, a piano, and certain tools. Together decide how objects will be treated and maintained to preserve enjoyment for all.

7. Because wives often complain about how their husbands leave the bathroom, the kitchen, or some other area, it is important for you to examine your own behavior in relation to your husband's domain, including his car, his office, his shop, and his bathroom.

∽ Week 4 ∾

Showing love, honor, and respect for God also means showing love, honor, and respect for our neighbors. This week's ideas will focus on specific ways to respect those outside our homes. John 3:16 reminds us that "God so loved the world that He gave His one and only Son." Loving our families means helping them grow in love and respect for others outside our own walls.

1. Teach your children to respect your neighbors' property by allowing them to go into their yard only with permission.

2. Make it a habit to promptly return items borrowed from others. This includes everything from library books to a neighbor's lawn mower.

3. Set a family standard of returning items in better condition, if at all possible, than when you borrowed them. For example, if you borrow a car or lawn mower, return it with a full tank of gasoline. If you borrow a camera, return it with a new roll of film.

4. Obey speed limits and parking ordinances as an example of what it means to respect the rules and boundaries of others.

5. Be prompt. Arriving at, or a little before, the appointed hour says you honor those waiting for you. It respects their time and wishes. This is one

area where a husband may especially appreciate his wife's efforts to respect his boundaries.

6. Care for your community by collecting trash left along the roadside or in public areas. Enlist the help of family members and friends as you all care for the rights of others.

7. Pay attention to your family's "noise level." Is your radio, stereo, or television disruptive to the neighborhood? How do the neighbors feel about your son's rock band playing in the garage? Will your daughter's slumber party disturb the people next door? Help your children learn to be sensitive to the needs and wishes of others.

5

EXPRESS LOVE
BY REMEMBERING
AND REFLECTING

The second Saturday in May they always appeared, side by side in the refrigerator, in perfect white boxes tied with gold cord. Sometimes they were roses, sometimes orchids. Always they were chosen to coordinate with dresses to be worn by my mother and grandmother the next day. They were one way my father annually honored both his wife and mother on Mother's Day. The regularity of this simple gift spoke volumes to me, my brother, and my sister. It reminded us of the importance of not only loving our mother, and communicating that on a regular basis, but also setting aside time to honor her on special occasions. It emphasized to us the importance of remembering.

Two weeks after this event came Memorial Day, a time when we honor those who have gone before us and given their lives fighting for our country. Because of them, we enjoy the freedoms we have today. Our farm family frequently spent the day making hay—it was that time of year in Missouri. But Mom always remembered to get out the flag and fly it from the front porch—no matter what we were doing. It made us reflect on where our freedom to make hay came from in the first place.

Hundreds of miles away, at the same time we were making hay, my husband's family in Michigan was enjoying a slightly different observance of the day. His family typically made their semiannual trek to the cemetery on Memorial Day. Flowers were placed on graves or planted in urns as people walked among the grave markers and talked quietly of those who had died. It was a day for remembering.

Today on Memorial Day, our family stands proudly along a curb in our hometown as local school bands march by playing patriotic tunes. The Veterans of Foreign Wars, Boy Scouts, Girl Scouts, and local dignitaries complete the solemn contingent. A lively cadence moves the group along, but each year everyone comes to a complete halt at the State Street bridge where the VFW bugler plays the lonely notes of "Taps." Then wreaths are tossed into the Kishwaukee River, which flows through our town. A 21-gun salute follows in honor of the soldiers who have not returned. It is a quiet, haunting moment that reminds us all of the debt that has been paid for our freedom. The Memorial Day commemoration closes with more stirring music, speeches, and prayers from the gazebo in Big Thunder Park.

Remembering, recalling, and respecting are vital to

families. We need these times when we touch our roots, connect with our past, and recall the hard work, courage, and dedication of those who have gone before us. We need these moments as inspiration for our future. Remembering the faithfulness of our ancestors encourages us to keep on in the ways God is directing us today.

Hebrews 11:1–12:3 speaks very clearly to this fact. Chapter 11 begins with its own biblical Memorial Day parade as it recites the faithfulness of God's people over thousands of years. As we read this role call of the faithful who trusted God despite extremely difficult circumstances, God works through His Word to send His Spirit to stir up similar trust and resolution in us. Life was difficult for these children of God, yet they continued to follow the Lord and await His promises.

> *Others were tortured and refused to be released, so that they might gain a better resurrection. Some faced jeers and flogging, while still others were chained and put in prison. They were stoned; they were sawed in two; they were put to death by the sword. They went about in sheepskins and goatskins, destitute, persecuted and mistreated—the world was not worthy of them. They wandered in deserts and mountains, and in caves and holes in the ground.*

> *These were all commended for their faith, yet none of them received what had been promised. God had planned something better for us so that only together with us would they be made perfect. (Hebrews 11:35–40)*

And what is the conclusion? What can be our goal and focus as we love our husband and children by helping them remember and reflect on what God has done? The writer of Hebrews gives us clear direction here:

> *Therefore, since we are surrounded by such a great cloud of witnesses, let us throw off everything that hinders and the sin that so easily entangles, and let us run with perseverance the race marked out for us. Let us fix our eyes on Jesus, the author and perfecter of our faith, who for the joy set before Him endured the cross, scorning its shame, and sat down at the right hand of the throne of God. Consider Him who endured such opposition from sinful men, so that you will not grow weary and lose heart. (Hebrews 12:1–3)*

The activities this month are designed to help your family remember those who have gone before them and reflect on how their faithfulness can be an encouragement to live for the Lord now. Each week has a slightly different emphasis, but all the activities are designed to help you become better acquainted with your family's origins and use them as a springboard for greater family faithfulness.

ᗡᗡ Week 1 ᗡᗡ

Remember Our Country's Heros

1. Attend a Memorial Day parade and talk about why we celebrate this holiday.

2. Fly a flag as a sign of respect for those who have died so that we might be free. Talk about how Jesus also gave His life that we could be free from sin, enjoy new life now, and live forever with Him in heaven.

3. Place flowers on the grave of a friend or relative. Help children count the number of flags in the cemetery. Talk about why we honor those who have gone before us.

4. Dig out the photo albums and show children pictures of family members who have died. For those pictures of living relatives, discuss the changes that have taken place. Talk about the stories of their lives—especially those who may have served in the armed services.

5. Attend a Memorial Day celebration. Listen to or read a patriotic speech and talk about the meaning of loyalty and allegiance.

6. Remember a veteran. As a family, send a personal thank-you note to someone who has fought in a war or served in the military. Include veterans

and people in the armed forces in your prayers.

7. Send a care package or cheerful note to someone you know who is away from home serving in the armed forces.

⬭ Week 2 ⬭

Recall Your Family's Heritage

1. Ask grandparents or other older extended family members to talk about their lives and especially about how they have seen God's hand at work.

2. Record memories and stories of older family members on audiocassette or videocassette or in written form.

3. Help children make a family tree. Elaborate diagrams, suitable for framing, may often be purchased in gift stores. To begin, you may choose to make a simpler design of your own for use with your children. A photocopied page from a baby book or Bible could be used.

4. Do a family genealogy project by researching a great-grandparent. Include stories about this individual for younger family members.

5. Reproduce old photos of your extended family to enhance a genealogy project. Pictures make the stories even more vivid. They also help children see family resemblances.

6. Take new photos of important "historic sites" for the family. These might include the church where Great-Grandma was baptized, the first house where Grandma and Grandpa lived after they were married, or the school a parent attended.

7. Use more recent family photo albums to point out resemblances between children and their extended family. Help them see how they have the "Bower height," the "Pattison eyes," or the "McDonald freckles." Seeing resemblances helps children understand that they belong, that there is a place where they fit just right.

8. Compare family members to extended family in a positive way. For example:

> *"You remind me of your great-aunt Linda. She had such a way with words."*
>
> *"You're every bit as talented as your dad was with a hammer and saw. I know he would be proud of you."*
>
> *"I wish your great-grandma could have heard you sing. She sang so beautifully, and your voice is just as special as hers."*

9. Talk about family traits in a positive light. For instance:

> *"The Baker clan really knows how to have a good time. They always have had a sense of humor."*
>
> *"You can always tell a Bergdorf. They've never met a stranger."*
>
> *People say the Phelps name is well-respected. You can trust someone from the Phelps family to be honest and trustworthy."*

Week 3

Explore Family and Ethnic Origins

1. Do some library research on the meaning and heritage of your family name and on your ethnic origins.

2. Put together a cookbook of favorite family recipes.

3. Celebrate your family's ethnic identity with a special dinner featuring foods from your country of origin. If your family combines a variety of ethnic origins, so much the better. Celebrate them all!

4. Get children involved in identifying and celebrating their cultural roots by allowing them to decorate for the dinner with place mats, name cards, etc., that feature artwork or pictures characteristic of a particular heritage. For instance, a child with a Germanic background might make tiny German flags to adorn the table. He could write the German names of particular foods on cards and place them near the dishes. The place mats or centerpieces could be pictures of Germany or Switzerland.

5. Show interest in your husband's family. Ask him questions about his upbringing, memories, and family traditions. Ask him what he'd like to pass

on to his children from his family of origin. Discuss how traditions from your families of origin impact the traditions you establish in your own family. Make specific plans with your husband to establish traditions important to him.

6. Send a greeting to your husband's parents. Let them know how much you appreciate the impact they have had on his life and your family life.

7. Keep in touch with your husband's extended family. Send them news of your own family—including pictures—especially if they live far away.

Week 4

Revive Your Spiritual Heritage

Adopted children often have a strong need and desire to know where they came from and who they are in terms of biological origins. Even though they may love their adoptive parents, they long to see someone who "looks like them" in terms of hair, facial features, and physical makeup. When reunited with biological siblings or relatives, they are often surprised to see they have similar gestures, habits, likes, and dislikes despite a different upbringing.

In much the same way, we as Christians are all adoptive children of our heavenly Father. Our new life with Him, given to us at our Baptism and a result of Jesus' saving action, allows us much more than our natural family could ever give us. God gives us His Spirit to enable us to follow His plan for our lives, use His resources as His children, and receive the inheritance in heaven He has promised us as His heirs. Characteristics of our old family origins are still there, but we are now truly forgiven children of a new family, and nothing can ever separate us from our divine Parent's love.

1. As a family, celebrate each member's reception into God's heavenly family with Baptism-birthday parties. Bake a cake, light a baptismal candle, and enjoy the goodness of God's family as you eat a meal together. Remember to celebrate your husband's Baptism birthday and your own.

2. Keep a baptismal birthday journal or photo album. Include photos from the baptismal day, cards or notes from sponsors over the years, and special thoughts you have recorded about your child's spiritual development.

3. Ask grandparents, special teachers, sponsors, and spiritual mentors to contribute to your child's baptismal journal. Let them know this will be presented to the child at his or her confirmation.

4. Present the baptismal album or journal to your child at his or her confirmation.

5. Give a small gift to your child on his or her baptismal birthday to symbolize membership in God's family.

6. Read Hebrews 11:1–12:3 together and talk about other family members listed here. Discuss how this "cloud of witnesses" encourages us as we live for Christ each day. For smaller children, drawing "cloud pictures" with faces in them may help them understand how we are surrounded and watched by those who have faithfully walked with the Lord.

7. Thank your husband often, including in front of your children, for being the spiritual head of your household and a faithful witness.

8. As a family, talk about the heritage we each will leave behind for those who will come after us. As a family, how would you like to be remembered? As a person, how would you like to be remembered? If you were to move today, what would your neighbors say about you after you were gone? Recognizing your uniqueness as individuals and as a family, how do you think God would want you to be remembered? How does God help you leave behind a heritage that honors Him?

9. If you haven't already done this, take time now to remember and reflect on the lives of extended family members who have left behind a godly heritage. Discuss how they did this and how God enabled them through His Holy Spirit to witness.

6

Express Love
by Celebrating
Commitment

"You guys aren't going to get a divorce, are you?"

The question certainly captured my attention. It had been one of those days when my husband and I weren't exactly arguing, but things were strained between us, and the friction must have been evident. All couples, even in good marriages, have these moments, so while it was unpleasant at the time, I wasn't particularly worried about the outcome. I knew we would reestablish our old rapport.

What surprised me was the impact our disagreement was having on our daughter! We had never mentioned the "D" word in our house in relation to our marriage. We didn't scream and yell at each other. We didn't argue on a routine basis, yet she was concerned about the temporary tension, and immediately her thoughts jumped to divorce. We hurried to reassure her that, as far as we were concerned, divorce was not an option. Mommy and Daddy might have disagreements, much as she and her brother might have fights and arguments, but we were not divorcing each other. We planned on staying together and working things out for a long time to come.

This little episode in our lives taught us how unfamiliar today's children are with the concept and experience of commitment. Not that long ago, when two people got married, they stayed married for life. When someone got a job just out of high school or college, he could be expected to have that same job three or four decades later. Promises made were promises kept, and loyalty to one's family, employer, and country meant something.

Charles Klein speaks to this problem in his book *How to Forgive When You Can't Forget:*

> *What is becoming frighteningly obvious is that some people believe that relationships are expendable and people are disposable. Living in a throw-away age, we have become accustomed to getting rid of that which is no longer functioning properly. We believe it's simpler and more convenient to replace than it is to repair. That philosophy may work well with coffee makers or toasters, but in real life, it destroys the way in which people relate to one another.*

In today's changing work force, men and women expect to change jobs, perhaps even careers, three or four times during their adult lives. Questioning one's government and leaders is valued more than expressing loyalty or patriotism. Families in particular suffer from the "commitment crisis," with half of all marriages in the last decade ending in divorce.

Children especially suffer from the lack of security and stability in relationships. According to Wallerstein and Blakeslee in *Second Chances: Men, Women and Children a Decade After Divorce,* the effects of divorce are often long lasting.

> *Children are especially affected because divorce occurs during their formative years. What they see and experience becomes a part of their inner world, their view of themselves, and their view of society. The early experiences in a failing marriage are not erased by divorce. Children who witnessed violence between their parents often found these early images dominating their own relationships ten and fifteen years later. Therefore, while divorce can rescue a parent from an intolerable situation, it can fail to rescue the children.*

The book goes on to note that children of divorced parents have a much higher incidence of divorce themselves. Certainly the experience of divorce and the resulting feelings of insecurity impact children for a long time.

Even if a child comes from a happy home with a stable marriage, he or she probably knows at least half a dozen other children whose mothers and fathers are not together any longer. Divorce has happened to others near to them. They have heard stories of "my weekend with Daddy" and "Mommy's new boyfriend"; they fear it could happen to them as well.

In a time when so many marriages have failed and divorce has wounded the heart of many a child, children need to be reassured that their home *will not fail*. As a wife and mother, you can reassure your child of the strength of your commitment to her father and your husband by honoring and celebrating the joys of marriage. You can show her what it means to be faithful in relationships by the loyalty and commitment you show to your husband, even when he is not feeling well or is acting in a way that upsets you. You can express commitment by continuing to work on resolving conflict in relationships, asking God's help as you go.

But what if you are not married because death or divorce has taken your husband? As a Christian mother you still have a powerful way to reassure your child, reminding her of God's unwavering commitment to us. You can talk about the frailty of human promises, admitting your own failures and at the same time stressing the certainty of God's love. Let her know that God has a special place in His heart for the widow and the orphan. Share with her one of the following Bible passages that emphasize God's special concern for the fatherless.

> *But You, O God, do see trouble and grief; You consider it to take it in hand. The victim commits himself to You; You are the helper of the fatherless. (Psalm 10:14)*

*A father to the fatherless, a defender of widows,
is God in His holy dwelling. (Psalm 68:5)*

*For the LORD your God is God of gods and
Lord of lords, the great God, mighty and awesome,
who shows no partiality and accepts no bribes. He
defends the cause of the fatherless and the widow,
and loves the alien, giving him food and clothing.
(Deuteronomy 10:17–18)*

The effect of divorce on children is enormous, but
the grace and mercy of God is even more powerful. No
matter what our marital state happens to be, ultimately
we need to point our children to the One who will
never fail them. We need to remind them that their
heavenly Father is eternally committed to their best
welfare. Knowing this, we then need to live out this
confidence as we walk each day with Him.

∞ Week 1 ∞

Celebrate Marriage

Children find great security in knowing their parents love each other. This week's suggestions are intended to reinforce the romantic love and long-term commitment of the marital relationship for you and for your children. If you are not married but have relatives or close friends (parents, sisters, brothers, or neighbors) who are married, you may want to modify some of these activities to include them. In families of divorce, it is especially important to help children know that lifelong marriages do occur and are considered the norm in God's eyes.

1. Get out your wedding pictures and relive the events of the day. Tell your children the funny and tender stories associated with the event.

2. Try on your wedding dress for husband and children to see. If it doesn't fit, at least let the children see the dress in which Mommy was married.

3. Make a specific point of talking to your children about your wedding rings. Show them the rings both Mommy and Daddy wear. Talk about what it means to exchange rings and wear a ring.

4. Recall the day you met your husband and your first impressions of each other. This can be a happy memory for a couple. It is also one chil-

dren usually find very interesting. Plan a surprise meal for your husband, commemorating your first date.

5. Recall the details of your engagement. Share these with your children if they are old enough to appreciate and understand.

6. Show the children a copy of your marriage certificate. Explain what is involved in getting a certificate and why the names of witnesses are included.

7. Talk about the wedding vows you spoke to your husband. Explain what they mean and why they are important. You might even want to do this over the space of a week, spending a day on each of the following phrases:

   ➤ For better, for worse

   ➤ For richer, for poorer

   ➤ In sickness and in health

   ➤ To love and to cherish

   ➤ Forsaking all others

   ➤ As long as you both shall live

8. Let your children hear you say "I love you" often to your husband.

9. Show your children by example that you and your husband value time spent together.

# Week 2

Celebrate Your Anniversary

Every June a small package mysteriously appeared for my mother from my father. It wasn't Mother's Day. It wasn't her birthday. It wasn't even their wedding anniversary. It was the anniversary of the day my father asked my mother to marry him and she said yes. My father chose to celebrate this event by honoring my mother each year with a small, personal gift. I doubt they thought much about it at the time, but this small practice spoke volumes to my brother, my sister, and me as we observed the fondness of our parents for each other.

Until one reaches the 25th year of marriage, anniversary celebrations are generally reserved for the couple alone as a reminder of the love they share and the commitment they have made to each other. Though you may not have thought of it before, celebrating romantic anniversaries has benefits beyond your own enjoyment. Just the fact that you make time for each other apart from your children helps emphasize to them the importance and stability of your marriage.

While each couple's preferences and tastes need to be considered—along with the money in their wallets—commemorating the day the two of you were joined as husband and wife is a powerful way to express committed love to your husband and your children. The following are some suggestions to help you do just that.

1. Women often expect their husbands to plan a romantic evening for them as their anniversary celebration. This year, try something different. Plan a wedding anniversary celebration for your husband with his likes and interests in mind. Express appreciation and affection to him for his faithfulness over the years.

2. Celebrate the day you met or became engaged. Surprise your husband with an unexpected gift or card on that date.

3. Renew your vows in church. Ask your pastor to help you plan the ceremony.

4. Place flowers on the altar in thanksgiving for God's continued blessing of your marriage.

5. Bake or buy a small wedding cake for a family celebration of your marriage. Most bakeries offer such a service as a way to "taste" their wares.

6. If you have a video or audio recording of your wedding, play it on your anniversary for each other and for your children.

7. Light a wedding candle on each of your anniversaries. Offer a prayer of thanksgiving.

Week 3

Make Promises

For two weeks we have been focusing on commitment in terms of the promises made between a husband and wife in marriage. While this is certainly an important part of the faithfulness God intends for us to have in marriage, it is not the only facet of committed love. In the coming week, activities will focus on steadfastness and loyalty in other contexts. Use these activities as a springboard to talk about commitment to one's self, one's family, one's neighbor, one's country, and most importantly, to God.

1. As a family, talk about the promises people make to each other. For example, a mother might promise to take her daughter shopping. A father might promise to take his children to the zoo. What does it mean to promise something? What kind of promises have you made?

2. When one appears in court as a witness, it is necessary to promise to "tell the truth, the whole truth, and nothing but the truth, so help me God." As a family, discuss why this promise is important. What kind of promises should we make to other people? What kind of promises should we avoid?

3. Engagement is a type of promise. As a family,

talk about what is meant by engagement. What kind of promise is this?

4. Many families and churches are asking teens to make a commitment to be pure, saving the sexual relationship until marriage. As a sign of this promise and commitment, parents give their child a ring, pin, or some kind of jewelry. If your children are old enough to understand this concept, talk about why it might be helpful to a young person.

5. If you have teenagers, consider giving them a special ring or other item of jewelry to reinforce the importance of sexual purity. Present it to them at a special dinner. An accompanying note or card may be especially meaningful.

6. In June, Americans celebrate Flag Day. When we say the Pledge of Allegiance, we are making a promise to honor our national flag and our country. Talk about what this commitment means.

7. If you don't already have one, buy a flag and fly it regularly to express your commitment to the country in which God has placed you.

Week 4

God's Promises

Human promises are fine and often well intentioned, but they do sometimes fail. Marriages dissolve. Homes fall apart. Witnesses lie in court. Citizens betray their country. When these things happen, our confidence is often shaken. We wonder if anything or anyone can remain sure and unshakable. This is precisely when we need God most. His promises are always sure. He *will* keep His word.

God knows our human weaknesses and our need for signs of His promises. Throughout Scripture He gives visual reminders of His faithfulness to His people. These signs comforted His people then, and they continue to comfort us today. The following week focuses on the sights and sounds of God's promises. Allow the Holy Spirit to work through these activities to give your family members the peace and security only God can give.

1. Read Genesis 9:12–16 and discuss the passage with your family. How is the rainbow a sign of God's love and faithfulness? What does He promise us here?

   Depending on the age of your children and their level of ability, draw or make rainbows to hang on the family bulletin board or in their rooms. In the coming week, use rainbow stickers on personal notes to each family member. Create a rainbow mobile to hang in a highly visible spot in your home.

2. Read Genesis 15:5; 22:17; and 26:4. Also read Hebrews 11:11–12. Discuss these passages with your family. How did God use stars as a sign of His covenant with Abraham? What are some of God's promises to us? Go outside and look up at the stars tonight and remind each other of God's continued faithfulness. Remind your children that many years after Abraham gazed at the stars, God sent His Son—a descendant of Abraham—to be our Savior.

3. Talk with your children about the cleansing power of water. In Baptism God uses simple means—water—to show that our sins are forgiven and we are washed clean. It is not the water alone but His Word with the water that changes us. Talk about the promises God gives you in Baptism and the vows you make to God. After talking about the wonderful ways God has used and continues to use water, go outdoors and run through the sprinkler or have a water fight as a family.

4. God knows that as humans we often need visible signs of His presence. Identify the common sign given in the following passages: Exodus 3:2; Exodus 13:21–22; and Acts 2:2–3. Ask your family why they think God uses this sign. Light a can-

dle, strike a match, or build a campfire. Talk about how God is like a fire and how we can remember His commitment to us when we see a fire.

5. Read Luke 1:26–38. Here the angel Gabriel brings news of a visible sign of God's love and faithfulness. What is it? How is this the most powerful of all God's signs? Sing "Away in a Manger," "O Little Town of Bethlehem," "Joy to the World," or some other Christmas carol to celebrate God's very personal sign to all creation.

6. Read Luke 22:14–20. As a family, discuss the story of the Last Supper. Here Jesus uses visible elements as a sign of His commitment to us. What are the two elements? How are they a sign of God's commitment to us? How are they like a wedding ring? How are they different?

7. Celebrate the Lord's Supper this Sunday with all confirmed members of your family. Take younger children to the Communion rail for a blessing.

7

EXPRESS LOVE
WITH FREEDOM
AND RESPONSIBILITY

I watched him walk off across the mall by himself. His blond head was now level with mine, and he walked with the confident swagger of a young adolescent. "Meet you in a couple of hours, Mom," he said. "Don't worry!"

I wasn't worried, exactly. I knew he didn't need me to follow him around the shopping center, but I could see by his growing independence that he needed me less and less every day to do the things I'd grown so good at doing. I knew how to take care of him, but he wanted to take care of himself. What had happened to that round-cheeked, blue-eyed toddler who eagerly climbed in my lap to listen as I read him the same story over and over and over again? Where was the little boy who had been fearful of the dark and his first swimming lessons? Where was the child who cried so easily when things didn't go well? He had been replaced by an eager-to-conquer-the-world adolescent. He had many lessons to learn, but he was sure he could master them all.

As his mother I had stopped holding his hand long ago. Now, most often, I found myself on the sidelines, correcting his occasional errors, encouraging his progress, and cheering his successes. My role had changed. While I was proud of the young man he was becoming, I still missed the little boy sometimes. Traces of sadness mingled with pride as I watched him stroll away. I sighed, knowing there would be many more times of watching him leave.

We need to begin to let our children go from the moment of birth, perhaps from the moment of conception—at least mentally and emotionally. They are gifts from God given to us for just a little while to love and to rear in ways that honor Him. It isn't easy. In the early days we wonder if we'll ever again sleep through the night without interruption. Sometimes we despair in the midst of tantrums and tears, thinking there must be a better mother for the job than ourselves. Our time is so tied to theirs that the engine of the car rarely cools before we're called on to car pool to yet another event. We become so attached to our offspring, and so good at caring for them, that we begin to think of them as ours. But they're not! They're on loan from God, and we must prepare them to live responsibly and independently.

Even Jesus' mother struggled with this. When He was just 12 years old, He accompanied His parents to Jerusalem, a city several day's journey from their hometown of Nazareth. Luke describes the conclusion of their visit like this:

> *After the Feast was over, while His parents were returning home, the boy Jesus stayed behind in Jerusalem, but they were unaware of it. Thinking He was in their company, they traveled on for a day. Then they began looking for Him among their relatives and friends. When they did not find Him, they went back to Jerusalem to look for Him. After three days they found Him in the temple courts, sitting among the teachers, listening to them and asking them questions. Everyone who heard Him was amazed at His understanding and His answers. When His parents saw Him, they were astonished. His mother said to Him, "Son, why have You treated us like this? Your father and I have been anxiously searching for You."*
>
> *"Why were you searching for Me?" He asked. "Didn't you know I had to be in My Father's house?" But they did not understand what He was saying to them. (Luke 2:43–50)*

The King James Version gives us a slightly different translation here, which helps guide our perspective of our own children. It says, "I must be about My Father's business" (Luke 2:49 KJV). Just as Mary was misguided in her understanding of what Jesus should be doing, so we also are sometimes misdirected in the dreams or ideas we have for our children. We try to hold onto them when we should be letting them go. We pull them back when we need to encourage them to go out a little farther. We impose our hopes and dreams on them when we need to allow them to develop the gifts God has given them.

Though He wasn't a parent, Jesus was a master teacher in allowing His own disciples freedom to grow and stretch, risk and fail. In Matthew 10 we see how Jesus sends out the Twelve, giving them authority to drive out evil spirits and the ability to heal every disease and sickness. Even though they did not fully comprehend who He was at this point, or why He had come, Jesus sent them out to do His work. What confidence He must have had in them! How thrilled they must have been to return and tell Him all that had happened. Mark 6:30 tells us that "the apostles gathered around Jesus and reported to Him all they had done and taught."

Our job as mothers is similar. We see our children as fellow believers, disciples of Christ. We teach them, prepare them, and then allow them to go on learning as they accomplish tasks on their own. In the early years, they return to us often for correction and approval. Later, they come back less frequently. Eventually they are on their own, guided by the same Holy Spirit as we are, children of the same heavenly Father. We are their encouragers and supporters, but if we've done our job correctly, they are able to go forward without us as we stand cheering in the wings.

How do we accomplish this awesome task of helping our children become independent, fully functioning adults? With love and prayer, of course, but family counselor Jean Lush maintains that teaching our child to work is also a critical component. In her book *Mothers and Sons*, she offers the following insight, "Little boys must be taught to work efficiently and to be productive in a competitive society. Their first boss is their mother. If she teaches them well, there is a good chance they'll be successful when they face the world on their own as adults."

She goes on to add that failure to accomplish this task can have a devastating impact on a boy's lifelong ability to function in the real world.

> *For many years as a family therapist, I counseled numerous unemployed men with families. ... Despite many job opportunities, these men couldn't hold a job. ... In all these cases, I consistently saw one common denominator: These men were never required to work around the house when they were growing up. They were never taught to responsibly and efficiently complete a chore.*

Although we might undervalue the importance of chores, especially given the amount of whining and complaining we deal with when we ask our children to do something, learning to work at home is important. According to Lush, it contributes to a child's ability to be other centered, that is to consider the needs of those beyond one's self. This is a critical characteristic of a competent, compassionate adult. She puts it this way:

> *I maintain that boys must be required to do*

chores for several reasons. When they are responsi-
ble for household duties, they learn to contribute to
the family as a team member. This type of coopera-
tion teaches them to be other-centered. If all their
activities are fun involvements focused strictly on
their own interests, they're likely to become self-
centered. Routine jobs build character and teach
children to be responsible to loved ones.

This month's ideas are designed to help you love your children as you encourage their independence and develop their ability to be responsible. If you are reading this chapter in July when we celebrate our country's independence, these suggestions will help you and your family value the responsible behavior freedom demands.

Food Preparation

1. Talk with your husband about the values he would like to see developed in your children through cooperative efforts to plan and make family meals. Getting his opinions and ideas first yields a stronger base for building responsibility in your children.

2. Children as young as 3 years of age can help prepare a meal. Very young children can wash fruits or vegetables. Slightly older children can scrape carrots, make simple sandwiches, or cut up fruit. Middle- to late-elementary-age children can bake simple cookies or cakes from mixes, while teens can take responsibility for making most of a family meal—providing they have had some training and supervision.

3. Give each child a specific task related to mealtime set-up or clean-up. Very young children can place napkins or silverware on the table. Elementary-age children can set the table, wipe it off, or wash the dishes. Teenagers can take responsibility for set-up and clean-up of an entire meal on selected days.

4. Teach elementary-age children about budgeting for food by involving them in the following:

➤ Clip coupons to be used at the grocery store.

➤ Keep a price book or log of prices for the most commonly used items, such as peanut butter, cereal, milk, juice, eggs, and bread.

➤ Look through weekly grocery-store advertisements to determine the good buys of the week.

5. Teach teenagers about budgeting for food by giving them a fixed amount of money for the meal they are to prepare. They must plan the menu and do the shopping within their budgeted amount.

6. Ask your husband to take an active role in meal preparation or clean-up as a role model for the children. Tell him how much you value his assistance and ask where he would like to be the most helpful.

7. Allow family members to plan and execute a family dinner party. A 5-year-old, assisted by Mom or Dad, could plan and help prepare a meal of hamburgers, carrot sticks, applesauce, milk, and cookies. Older children and adults can plan meals around a special theme such as "Western Night," "Oriental Night," or "Cajun Night."

∞ Week 2 ∞

Household Chores

Another area where responsibility must be learned involves home maintenance and housecleaning. Children are rarely enthused about such tasks, but they continue to be necessary responsibilities. Coordinated and supervised wisely, household chores offer excellent opportunities for children to grow and mature in their ability to work cheerfully.

In *Money Matters for Parents and Their Kids*, Ron and Judy Blue offer the following perspective: "Children can be taught to make the bed, but they haven't been trained to make the bed until they make it correctly, voluntarily, with no nagging or demand that they do so."

In the upcoming week you'll have the chance to focus on these areas of responsibility, using the suggestions given below.

1. Make a game of routine household tasks, such as changing the sheets on the beds, emptying trash cans, dusting furniture, folding laundry, and the like. Challenge family members to see who can do their job the quickest, the neatest, or in the most creative manner.

2. Put on some snappy march music while the family is working together on a home-maintenance or housecleaning project. Put some fun and humor into cleaning the garage, picking up the

living room, or washing windows.

3. Offer a family reward for completing a joint project, such as "We'll all go swimming as soon as the yard work is done." Make sure everyone has a job he or she can successfully complete.

4. Give a blue-ribbon award for work well done. Judge for the "cleanest room," "neatest closet," or "tidiest toy shelf."

5. Break down large tasks into smaller, manageable pieces for young children. Instead of telling a child to clean his room, explain and model tasks like these:

   ➤ Picking up dirty clothes and putting them in the laundry basket.

   ➤ Picking up trash and putting it in the trash can.

   ➤ Putting books and magazines on the shelf.

   ➤ Putting toys back into the toy box.

   Check the child's work after each step and offer encouragement and praise. Finish each task until all the work is completed.

6. Don't expect your husband to supervise and be the heavy for all the work responsibilities given to your children. Talk together about the consequences of unfinished work and follow through as necessary.

7. Follow through with logical or natural consequences when chores are left undone. Natural consequences are those that typically occur when an action isn't completed. For example, your child has to sleep on a bare mattress because the sheets are not put back on the bed. Logical consequences are those that make sense, such as no television until a certain task is completed.

# Week 3

Prepare for Financial Freedom

According to Ron and Judy Blue, authors of *Money Matters for Parents and Their Kids,* one of the biggest mistakes parents can make in training children to manage money is not allowing them to fail. They suggest following these four principles when working with children.

- They must experience what is being taught.
- They must have an opportunity to fail.
- They must have feedback.
- They must have rewards.

It will be helpful to keep these four points in mind as you consider this week's activities.

1. Decide with your husband the portion or percentage of your family budget you will spend on church offerings, clothing, food, recreation, housing, and so on. Honor your husband by staying within the spending guidelines you set.

2. Teach your children about stewardship, that is, the concept that all that we have belongs first and foremost to God. Talk about how He wants us to manage or care for what He has given us. Be an example of a good steward in your generosity to others, especially those less fortunate. Let your children know that you regularly set aside money for the Lord's work. Help them do the same with

what you give to them and what they earn.

3. Beginning at 4 or 5 years of age, give your children a small amount of money to manage each week. Increase the amount as children grow and make them more responsible for financial decisions about school supplies, clothing purchases, recreational choices, and the like.

4. Beginning at about age 9 or 10, tell your children the amount of money you have set aside, as a family, for clothing purchases. When shopping, allow them some freedom in comparison shopping for various purchases. Help them compare the value of a T-shirt or pair of jeans purchased at a discount store, resale shop, or yard sale versus ones purchased at a trendy department store.

5. Talk with your children about the percentage of your income you plan to spend on recreation. Explain what this means—what items are covered in this category. For instance, you might include snacks and treats away from home as well as vacations and outings in this category. Allow each child over the age of 7 or 8 recreational money that they must budget. To be most effective, do *not* give in to begging, pleading, and whining when the child's recreational money runs out before the next pay period. (This is especially likely to occur when friends are buying treats and your child has already used up his or her money.)

6. By the time your child becomes a young teenager, he or she is capable of earning money from jobs such as baby-sitting and lawn mowing. Help your child open a checking account and/or savings account and master the mechanics of check writing and balancing an account.

Week 4

Learn to Make Wise Decisions

In *Money Matters for Parents and Their Kids*, the Blues offer thoughts on one more area crucial to healthy growth and development—decision-making. They explain that mastering the skills of decision-making will help your children enjoy freedom and security as adults. This week's ideas are selected to assist you in discussing decision-making with your husband and in teaching your children wise decision-making skills.

1. As a couple, choose a decision you need to make in the near future (buying a car, purchasing home furnishings, planning a vacation) and take time to examine options in a detailed way. Ask yourselves the following questions, which the Blues suggest discussing: What am I really trying to accomplish by making this decision? What is the best use of money, time, and talents? Are there other alternatives? And you will want to add a fourth question: Is my decision God pleasing?

2. Use the questions with your children to help them learn about the decision-making process, as well as to help them make a specific decision. For example, with a young child, you may only use the second question when determining the relative value of one toy against another. A 9- or 10-year-old might use the second and third questions for making larger purchasing decisions,

such as a bicycle. All three questions could be used to help a child age 10 and up determine whether to be involved in a particular activity, such as basketball or hockey, soccer or ballet lessons. In every case, model Christian decision-making with your children. Pray for God's guidance and blessing on your decision. Turn to His Word to seek His advice.

3. For larger, long-term decisions, help your child write out responses to the decision-making questions. Consider going with your child to discuss the decision with a mature Christian friend.

4. Show your children how you and your husband explore factors in complex choices. For instance, transportation may be the need, but several other factors, such as gas mileage, safety features, availability of service, and cost, enter into the decision of which car to purchase. Number various objectives in order of importance as you make a decision.

5. Help your child rank priorities for a decision she needs to make. For example, help her decide what she hopes to gain from deciding to be on a summer baseball team. What will this allow her to do? What will it prevent her from doing? What are her goals and objectives for the summer? How will being on a baseball team help her meet these goals? (This is an excellent process for you to use in deciding how many activities you will allow your children to participate in.)

6. Help your child see that making one choice necessarily means excluding others. None of us can have everything we want. Refuse the urge to allow your child to "have it all." It will set up false expectations for adulthood.

7. When it is safe to do so, allow your child to experience failure by making poor choices. Poor choices made in childhood are usually small choices, but they can be powerful teachers. They will help your child avoid negative consequences from damaging choices later in life.

8

EXPRESS LOVE THROUGH FAMILY VACATIONS

"I'm tired. Let's go back to the hotel."
"I'm thirsty. Can't we have something to drink?"
"My feet hurt. Let's find a place to sit down."

We were experiencing what most Americans view as the ultimate family vacation, but everyone was miserable. I wondered how we could be in the midst of one of America's most frequented family vacation spots and be so unhappy. Had other families had dismal Walt Disney World experiences, or were we the only ones?

The subject of family vacations stirs up mixed emotions in people. It is one thing to look forward to time away from work and routine responsibilities. It is quite another to negotiate and tolerate the tension that constant togetherness often inspires. Given the energy expenditure involved, as well as the financial commitment required, some might even wonder whether vacations are worth the effort. Isn't it easier and simpler to stay home? What makes a vacation worthwhile, anyway? Consider the following factors.

Perhaps the first thing to remember is that all family vacations do not require hours together in an automobile. Some of the best "vacations" may occur in the backyard or close to home. They allow uninterrupted family time apart from regular routine. When children are young, these briefer, less-expensive outings provide enjoyable memories.

One family made a habit of taking picnic lunches to the park in a neighboring community where they made periodic shopping trips. Their preschool children enjoyed the novelty of eating outdoors as well as the adventure of using unfamiliar playground equipment. The parents enjoyed a relaxed meal away from the phone. These "homemade vacations" laid an important foundation for the children and helped them understand that fun does not have to cost money. They began to learn the possibilities of creating one's own entertainment.

As children grow, and finances allow, longer vacations may be possible and more enjoyable. These need to be planned carefully and take into account the energy levels and interests of the whole family. Some families enjoy camping. Others prefer saving for a ski trip in the winter. A week or two at a lake-side cottage is a treat for many, while others enjoy the novelty of visiting various historic sites and natural wonders. Whatever choice is made, parents need to consider the opportunities each site allows for shared experiences and memories. In their "Love Is a Decision" seminars, Gary Smalley and John Trent describe the powerful bonding that occurs as families share good times and bad. It's amazing how frequently both of these qualities are intertwined in a family vacation.

When I was 10 years old, my family took a camping vacation from southern Missouri to Washington D.C. For weeks my mother worked at sewing the canvas portion of our homemade camper. It even had upholstered cushions and netted screens. My father built the chassis, which had room for the five of us to sleep, eat, and store our clothing. The preparations were completed by early August, and we embarked on our first camping adventure.

How excited we all were! The first night we made it as far as eastern Kentucky where we set up camp just before a thunderstorm of biblical proportions broke loose. My sister got lost in the dark on the way back from the rest room. Our camper leaked most of the night, and three of us ended up sleeping in our little Ford Fairlane. When the sun came out the next morning, we dried ourselves as best we could, donned our Sunday clothes, and headed to church. In the afternoon, we found a Laundromat and dried our clothing while we opened up the tent to dry. Fortunately, the weather was more cooperative the rest of the trip.

We still laugh about that trip's damp beginning. My mother is certain my sister and I missed most of the Blue Ridge Mountains because we were arguing over Barbie dolls in the backseat. No doubt it was stressful for my parents to travel with three grade-school-age children, but my brother, sister, and I all have fond memories of that trip. We probably couldn't tell you about anything in particular that happened the remainder of the summer, but we do recall, with laughter and affection, our family camping adventure.

Family vacations provide bonding experiences that build cornerstones for significant life events. On our family's first outing to Colorado, my father decided we should all go hiking. My mother was dubious, but my sister and I were not to be discouraged. We set out with Dad, hoping to climb above the tree line before noon and eat our sack lunch at the summit. As we climbed, Dad's calls of encouragement rang in our ears. "This ain't no hill for a stepper!" he joked in his Ozark dialect. We loved his positive attitude and scrambled to keep up.

By noon we were definitely above tree line and nearing the summit, so we stopped to eat the sandwiches Mom had packed. We girls were ravenous, but Dad didn't look too hungry. He nibbled a bit at his lunch but mostly sat and rested.

Soon storm clouds began to gather, and Dad decided we needed to get out of the open country where lightening might strike us. We stuffed our sandwich bags in our pockets as the wind rose. About that time an experienced hiker came over the summit from the other side of the mountain and hiked with us. The hiker chatted about the weather and the route, but our father was unusually quiet. As we reached the bottom and the clouds let loose, drenching us with torrents of rain, our new friend offered to give us a ride to our campsite. My father encouraged my sister and me to take advantage of his thoughtfulness, but my father politely refused the ride, saying he preferred to walk.

Only later did we discover that our "stepper" father had experienced altitude sickness and lost the contents of his stomach at the bottom of the mountain. Apparently climbing a mountain takes some conditioning when one is unaccustomed to the altitude. For years after that, whenever one of us faced a large obstacle, someone in the family was sure to say, "That ain't no hill for a stepper!" It still makes us laugh, but we learned it is best to be prepared for challenges.

Vacations allow your family to get away from the routine and rest. Vacations offer time to relax mentally as well as physically. Jesus recognized this and frequently took time away from the demands of public ministry to rest, reflect, and pray to His Father. He also recognized His disciples' need for rest and at times invited them to come away from the crowds. On one occasion, He sent out the Twelve two-by-two to visit various villages, preaching the kingdom of God and healing the sick. When they returned, the disciples were eager to tell Jesus all that had happened. Because they seemed so invigorated from their experiences, one might have expected Jesus to give them a brief pep talk and send them on their way again. Surprisingly, He did something different! "When the apostles returned, they reported to Jesus what they had done. Then He took them with Him and they withdrew by themselves to a town called Bethsaida" (Luke 9:10).

Could it be that our Lord understands us better than we understand ourselves? Perhaps He sees clearly that our need to rest is sometimes greater than our need to keep going. Psychologist Dr. Archibald Hart offers some critical insights on the importance of rest and slower-paced living in his book *Stress and Your Child.* He notes that fast-track living is hard on both parents and children, but fast-track parents can still be excellent parents if they devote time and attention to their children's needs. Because this may mean some dramatic changes in attitudes and behaviors, Dr. Hart offers the following five suggestions:

- Remind yourself and your child to slow down.
- Plan activities that involve the whole family and that help you focus on process, not goals.
- Create "quiet times" for both yourself and other family members.
- Above all else, protect your family's free time.
- Give absolute priority to your family commitments.

Dr. Hart completes his thoughts by saying:

> *Every child deserves some long ice-creamy afternoons. Every child should know the smell of new-mown grass and feel the dew on naked feet. Every child should hear stories of your childhood adventures or your travels,*

about your parents and grandparents and times gone by. Every child should know the comfort of lounging with the family by the fireplace on a cold winter night.

If these are the kinds of memories you want to give your child and share with your husband, then the suggestions for this month should help. Why not choose some "close to home" ideas to use right away!

∽ Week 1 ∽

In the Backyard

1. Spread blankets or sleeping bags on the ground in the backyard. Have family members lay on their backs, look up at the stars, and talk about the greatness of God's creation. To close the evening, read Genesis 15:5–6 where God brought Abraham outside to view the stars and promised him more descendants than he could count. Try the same activity when you can be alone with your husband for a few minutes.

2. Have a family campout in the backyard. Even though the neighbors may think you're strange and your beds inside are more comfortable, young children are not likely to forget the night you "ate out" and "slept out." Talk together, tell stories, and fall asleep in the same tent!

3. Run through the sprinkler or have a water fight. Surprise your family by allowing the "kid" in you to have fun in an undignified way. Surprise your husband with kid-like behavior too!

4. Have a family water balloon toss. Invite neighborhood children to participate if you like. This is a cool activity for a hot day.

5. Make homemade ice cream. Borrow an ice-cream freezer if you don't have one. If you happen to

use a hand-crank model, so that everyone has to take turns turning the handle, so much the better.

6. Plan a "funny photo day." Encourage creativity in your children and husband by allowing them to be photographed in clothing and positions they find amusing, for example, wearing funny hats or hanging upside-down in a tree. When the pictures have been developed, display them in a prominent place and allow friends and family members to vote for the "funniest," "most creative," and "goofiest."

7. Increase your family's perceptive abilities by planning a family scavenger hunt. Scout the neighborhood in advance and then give each team a list of questions to be answered by scouring the neighborhood. Be sure to match an adult or older child with young children and review safety rules. Questions might include the following:

> ➤ How many shutters are on the house on the corner of 2nd and Main?

> ➤ What color are the flowers in Mrs. Malone's front yard?

> ➤ What is sitting on the front porch of the house at 6564 Maple Street?

> ➤ How many street signs can be found between Beech and Oak streets?

Set a time limit for each team. The losing team

has to treat the winning team at a local ice-cream parlor.

8. Spend the afternoon with your daughter and her friends. Dress up in old dresses from your own wardrobe, yard sales, or second-hand stores. Add jewelry, do everyone's hair, apply makeup, and take pictures! Complete the afternoon with a real tea party using the good dishes. (This is probably a good day to send the guys fishing or hiking.)

∞ Week 2 ∞

Close to Home

1. Take a picnic supper to the park. Spend a leisurely evening eating, talking, and playing together. Allow unhurried time for younger children to enjoy the playground equipment. This is a simple activity, yet one frequently overlooked by young parents.

2. Schedule a date with your husband for an evening picnic or an outdoor concert.

3. Visit a planetarium. As a family, learn to identify various constellations.

4. Visit a zoo. Take pictures of family members near their favorite animal. A trip to the public library after the zoo can help children learn more about animals they found especially intriguing. It presents a good opportunity to encourage an interest in learning for the sake of learning.

5. Check out local museums and historical societies. Help family members get a sense of local history. Some communities offer brochures with directions for cemetery walks and driving tours of the area. These activities can help you gain an appreciation for the original settlers of your communty.

6. Spend the day at a community pool or area lake. Build sand castles. Have inner tube races. Play in

the water. Splash each other. Relax and enjoy each other's company.

7. Check out area forest preserves or conservation districts. Many offer seasonal programs on vegetation and wildlife with special features for children and adults. Nature programs can form the basis for further reading, collections, and explorations.

8. Attend community concerts in the park. During the summer months, many areas feature free musical events for the whole family. Take a blanket or lawn chairs and spend the evening enjoying your favorite music. These are often ideal places to expose young children to different kinds of music because the concerts are free and people can come and go during the evening. That means you can adjust your stay to the attention span of your children.

9. Plan a weekend getaway with your husband or better yet, surprise him! Most hotels offer special weekend packages, or check into a bed-and-breakfast within a half day's drive of your home. Spend the weekend relaxing. Eat breakfast in bed, take long walks, snuggle!

∽ Week 3 ∽

On the Road

Traveling can be difficult for parents and children. Confinement in the car, compounded by the length of travel, can equal frazzled nerves and testy temperaments. The following suggestions are meant to help families look forward to time spent together in the car.

1. In advance, pick a book you will read to your family while you travel. Choose one with several chapters that can be read over a period of time. Reading can be soothing, especially when traffic is snarled or when several hours remain before stopping for the night. If reading makes you car sick, play books on tape to hold the family's interest. These can generally be obtained from the public library. *Little Visits on the Go* (Concordia, 1992) is a book/audiocassette collection of devotions about traveling. It's a good resource for families with young children.

2. Prepare low-fat, easy-to-eat munchies for the car. Grapes, pretzels, and carrot sticks help quiet hunger pangs and ease boredom with little mess or expense.

3. Sing silly songs. Allow children to suggest and lead their favorites. Adults can teach children new songs—songs they may remember from their childhood. Car time is also a good time to

sing Christian hymns and songs that you want your children to remember.

4. Count out-of-state license plates. Keep a list and see how many facts you can record about a state—the state's capital, location, primary industry, most famous site, and biggest city.

5. Help children keep a vacation journal in a spiral notebook. Add postcards or brochure photos you have collected along the way to illustrate your day's activities. Even young children can enjoy this activity with a parent's help. Don't forget to record your child's words or thoughts about the day. If children have difficulty knowing what to write, ask them to complete a sentence you start, such as one of these:

➤ My favorite part of today was ...

➤ If I could repeat one part of today, it would be ...

➤ The thing I'll remember most is ...

Leave places in the journal so personal photos can be added later. Vacation journals make priceless family keepsakes. They are a nice way to wrap up a day, and they have the added advantage of being almost completed when the family gets home.

6. If the trip is a long one, plan to give out little surprises throughout the trip. Distribute them when family members are growing cross, impatient, or

irritable. New crayons, small books, travel games, and tiny toys can be packed in small plastic bags and distributed as needed. Don't forget to surprise your husband with some special treats he enjoys. Ask the kids to help you plan surprises for Dad.

7. Play the alphabet game. Look for sequential letters of the alphabet in road signs and billboards. To make the game more challenging, each letter must begin the word, not simply be contained in it. For example, *a* in *Appleton*, *b* in *Bayou*, and *c* in *children*.

∽ Week 4 ∽

Natural Wonders and Historical Sites

Do a little advance preparation on historical sites you plan to visit. It will make the trip more enjoyable and interesting.

1. Write or call the state's tourism commission. Request information on the areas you intend to visit. This free information will give you some idea of what attractions are available, as well as the ones that will be appropriate and interesting for your family.

2. Visit the public library with your children to research the history of a particular area. Which Native American tribes lived in the area? What historical events took place in the locality you plan to visit? What famous people lived there? What is the native plant life and vegetation? How is it different from the area where you live? Select age-appropriate books—both fiction and nonfiction—to heighten interest in the visit. A librarian can help you find children's fiction set in many places you might visit.

3. Take advantage of programs offered by park rangers and guides. Children may not always appear interested at the time but will often reflect on what they have learned.

4. If your budget is limited, allow each child to choose one special activity for the trip. For instance, one child may want to go horseback riding, while another chooses canoeing. Encourage family members to cooperate with each other's choices because each person will get a turn for his or her favorite activity.

5. Give your husband some time off. Make sure he can relax without feeling responsible for keeping the family happy. More than likely, he will appreciate this kindness so much he will want to return the favor!

Romantic Outings and Interludes

1. For the couple with young children and a limited budget, an evening "in" is often easier to plan than one away from home. Surprise your husband by arranging for the children to spend the evening with friends or family members. Or you could put them to bed early. Then spread a blanket and pillows on the floor in the living room or cuddle up on the couch. Light candles. Play romantic music. Rent a movie you'll both enjoy. Order pizza or plan an indoor picnic for two. These interludes for two can refresh romantic sparks that grow dim in the exhausting demands of caring for young children.

2. Meet your spouse for lunch. Bring along some of his favorites foods and take time to talk about

something besides the bills, the kids, and the to-do list. Enjoy each other's company!

3. After years of marriage, couples tend to think they know each other so well that they may lose the excitement and anticipation of being together. Add interest and energy to your relationship by doing something new together. Plan an unexpected outing or activity.

> Visit a forest preserve, state park, or conservation area together. Photograph new or interesting sights. Learn new information together.

> Try a new outdoor activity—bicycling, canoeing, cross-country skiing, hiking, or orienteering.

> Learn a new skill together—square dancing, line dancing, ballroom dancing, stained-glass making, painting, or woodworking.

> Break out of the TV rut by playing a game just for two people—cribbage, Chinese checkers, or chess.

> Visit an unfamiliar restaurant. Order something new from the menu. If you have this planned in advance and take care of the check yourself, your husband may enjoy himself even more.

4. Ask your husband to describe his idea of the perfect day or evening for two. Get his ideas of what he would enjoy and plan accordingly. (This is

important because women often give the kind of love they would like to receive, which is frequently different from what their husbands would like to experience.) It's important to honor your partner's ideas and preferences. Doing so helps him know he is acceptable to you.

2
Express Love by Learning Together

Because my husband is an elementary school principal, we are probably more invested in the educational process of our children than some parents. This doesn't mean our children have always done what we wanted or represented our values in a way that gives credit to our parenting skills. More likely, in the process of teaching our children and helping them learn and grow to mature adults, we have learned more than they. Our children have shown us how little we do know and how much we have yet to learn.

Parents sometimes make the mistake of thinking a child's education begins with formal schooling in preschool or kindergarten. They assume the teacher has a body of knowledge that he or she will impart to their child because children of a certain age group are supposed to know such things. Learning, in their minds, occurs at school. Play and relaxation happen at home.

Unfortunately, this train of thought is detrimental to parent and child. If we are to prepare our children to be lifelong learners, interested in and curious about the world in which they live, we need to cultivate that attitude in ourselves and our offspring both before our children begin formal education and while they are engaged in it. Cheri Fuller emphasizes this point in her book *Home-Life: Preparing Your Child for Success at School.*

Psychologist Dr. Charles Gouaux of Gouaux Clinical Associates, St. Louis, Missouri, has said that one of the most powerful things a parent can do to enhance, strengthen, and support his child's education is to let the child see him enjoying his own curiosity, using and expanding his intellect, and learning from new experiences. As you love learning, your child learns to enjoy his own curiosity, intellect, creativity, and talent. He becomes, in fact, a lifelong learner.

How does this happen? Many times it occurs naturally as parents interact with their children over life events. When our children were 4 and 5 years old, a friend of the family died. Because he had experienced a number of deaths in his immediate family as a child, my husband, Paul, thought it a good time for our children to learn about death, grief, and life in heaven. In some ways this would be a "gentler" lesson because our friend was not as close to the children as a family member would have been. Paul took them to the visitation at the funeral home. Together they viewed the body in the casket. Together they spoke to the widow. My husband explained that Ray was no longer in his body but lived in heaven with the Lord.

Andrew and Miriam seemed to take the whole thing matter of factly, and my husband felt pleased he had decided to take them along. Imagine his surprise when Miriam mused, "I wonder what it's like to have worms in your mouth!" What an opportunity he had to correct any faulty impressions she had and to reassure her again that when we die, we do not stay in our dead bodies, which are put into the ground. Rather, because Jesus died and rose for us, God takes us to be with Him in heaven and on the Last Day will give us glorified bodies. Miriam was satisfied, and Paul was happy to have the opportunity to correct her thinking.

My husband's experience with our children points to a very important concept that Cheri Fuller explains in her book:

> Many of the pleasures of learning and living come from relationships with other people. A child will be receptive to the teacher's teaching only if he has learned to care about the adults in his world. This kind of caring grows out of his own experiences of being cared about and respected and enjoyed.

Taking the time to investigate new experiences with our children—answering their questions and listening to their responses—gives them the feeling that they matter, that their thoughts and ideas are important, that their inquiries are worthy of response, that their curiosity and creativity are to be valued. This can occur during carefully constructed outings, such as trips to the zoo or museum, or happen naturally and spontaneously at the kitchen sink, in the car, or walking around the neighborhood.

Moses understood that all time spent with children is learning and growing time, and he wasn't even running a car pool or trying to negotiate today's busy schedules! Consider his words in Deuteronomy 6:6–9:

These commandments that I give you today are to be upon your hearts. Impress them on your children. Talk about them when you sit at home and when you walk along the road, when you lie down and when you get up. Tie them as symbols on your hands and bind them on your foreheads. Write them on the doorframes of your houses and on your gates.

When we help our children learn about life, we can also help them see God's hand in it. As we notice the beauties of nature, we can thank God for what He has done in it. As we investigate the intricacies of words and language, we can acknowledge God as the Maker of all people and the Creator of languages. The study of mathematics can emphasize God's orderliness. Music, drama, and art all express God's creativity. All of life can be seen as an opportunity to learn more about our heavenly Father and His handiwork.

This month's ideas are designed to help you take advantage of all the teachable moments your children give you. Some will help you construct times of learning—taking a trip to the zoo, touring a historical site, or visiting a conservation district. Others will assist you in being more in tune with the day-to-day opportunities that occur at home, in the car, while shopping, or during routine tasks. Finally, some suggestions are intended for you and your husband. Relationships need the freshness of new ideas and experiences. Thinking of your marriage as an opportunity for "continuing education units" will open your eyes to many possibilities for growth as a couple.

Week 1

Reading

One of my favorite books about the importance of reading is *The Read-Aloud Handbook* by Jim Trelease. Along with giving parents long lists of books they can read aloud to children, Jim notes the importance and value of such experiences. He points out that "reading aloud strengthens children's reading, writing, and speaking skills—and thus the entire civilizing process."

Trelease also stresses the importance of imitation. Children who see their parents read, and hear their parents read aloud to them, are more likely to enjoy reading themselves. Since parents serve as the primary role models in their child's language development, reading aloud plays a critical role in the development of a child's verbal skills.

Beginning the practice of reading aloud with young children helps prevent the "reading is work" phenomenon that often occurs once a child has entered school. Because reading is taught in school and the impression is sometimes given that learning is a child's work, some children never learn to read for pleasure. Reading aloud with children establishes the idea that reading is enjoyable—an event to which we can look forward.

According to Trelease, reading aloud to children also stimulates their interest, their emotional development, and their imagination. In addition, it's inexpensive and fun. As proof of the power of reading aloud, he offers the following anecdote.

More than half a century ago there was a poor Quaker woman who took in a foundling child and began reading Dickens to him every night. Surely she could not have dreamed the words and stories would have such an enormous impact; the boy, James Michener, would write his first book at age 39 and his thirty-second at 78. In between there would be best-sellers translated into 52 languages, selling more than 60 million copies, and enjoyed by countless millions of readers.

We may not all be mothers of great writers, but we surely can teach our children the joy of reading.

1. Visit the local public library on a regular basis. Allow your children to choose books for themselves as well as choosing special ones you will read to them.

2. Make visiting the library a family trip so your children see you and your husband enjoying books. Vary your interests from time to time. Include biographies, fiction, nonfiction, and even books for younger readers on your book list. I first read the Narnia chronicles by C. S. Lewis as an adult, and then I read them again to my children.

3. Build a home library of favorite books to be opened and shared again and again. Choose books with good illustrations and readable print.

4. Set aside time every day for reading aloud, even if it's only 10 or 15 minutes. With younger children this might be done at naptime in the afternoon or at bedtime in the evening. Older children can be read to after supper, before the table is cleared, while the dishes are being done, or when homework is finished in the evening. The important thing is that a regular time is established and becomes a habit for the family. Make sure older children get a chance to read aloud too. It provides good reading practice and gives you the opportunity to praise your child and encourage an enjoyable pastime. The best time might be as you wash dishes, do the ironing, or engage in any other usually mind-numbing task.

5. Choose a special book for a family vacation or lengthy car trip. We have driven hundreds of miles and reduced irritability dramatically, even into our children's teenage years, because I read to the family as we traveled.

6. If you cannot read inside a moving vehicle, consider using books on tape. Many selections can be found in your public library.

7. Read a book with your husband. For fun you might choose an adventure or mystery novel. For increased knowledge and self-improvement you might choose an interesting nonfiction book. Let your children hear you discussing favorite books.

Tell them about books you loved as children.

8. When you and your husband take turns reading a book, highlight favorite passages and write notes to one another. Exchanging the book and reading the other's comments can be enlightening as well as a good source of conversation starters. My husband and I have found this method helpful when reading a book about marriage or parenting together.

∽ Week 2 ∽

Writing

The love of reading often leads to an interest in writing. Because writing skills are key to expressing one's self in many areas of life, helping your child grow in this area is critical. The following suggestions are just a few of the endless possibilities. Build on these simple ideas to further encourage your family members to develop their writing skills.

1. Before young children are able to write much more than their names, you can encourage writing ability by writing for them. One way we did this was to allow Miriam and Andrew to make their own books about trips and outings. We saved pictures and postcards of places we visited. While the experience was still fresh in the children's minds—usually before bedtime that same day—I simply asked them to dictate text about the day's experience. Sometimes they drew illustrations and selected postcards and pictures to match their stories. These keepsakes made a wonderful record of our family outings and encouraged writing skills.

2. Once your children are old enough to write simple sentences, encourage them to write letters to grandparents or other family members who may live far away. If you choose a relative who is like-

ly to write back, your child will have additional reinforcement to continue the writing experience. If you and your husband take business trips, develop the habit of sending postcards home. Help your children write postcards when you are on vacation.

3. Make your own greeting cards for holidays in addition to Christmas. Let your child write his or her own text, especially for birthdays or holidays such as Mother's Day, Father's Day, and Grandparent's Day. Don't expect a young child to write an overwhelming number of valentines or Christmas cards.

4. Help your child develop a pen-pal relationship. Some pen-pal acquaintances continue into adult life. A pen pal gives your child an opportunity to practice writing skills, while building a friendship and learning about a different part of the world.

5. Keep a folder of special letters, papers, poems, and stories written by your child. Valuing her work in this way helps her understand that you think it's important.

6. Keep a family journal. Purchase a date book with wide spaces by each day. In the spaces, record a few sentences about the day's events. Entries might include these: "The crabapple trees bloomed today. It seems like they are later this

year." Or "Marcy had her first piano recital and did a great job. She played 'The Fiddler's Jig.' " Allow each family member to make an entry for the day.

7. If you are a good writer yourself, be careful how you critique your child's or your husband's writing. Encourage and support them by using a gentle touch when correcting errors and offering ideas for improvement.

Math and Science

Math was not one of my favorite subjects, nevertheless I generally did well in math class. I attribute my success in mathematics to my father. He helped me have a positive attitude toward difficult subject matter, and he stretched my abilities by offering additional problems of his own. He also encouraged me by helping me see math as a challenge and a game rather than a curse and drudgery. In short, he was *involved* with my math homework, whether he was helping me memorize multiplication tables or looking over my algebra homework. His positive attitude and interest helped me form a positive outlook.

Perhaps it was this same ability to enjoy learning that attracted me to my husband. He enjoyed math, but biological sciences were his specialty. At lunch one day, Paul described the structure of the celery I was eating. Walking around campus, he identified flowers and trees and described their characteristics and habitats. In an outdoor setting, he was always curious about the plants and animals living there. He expanded my world by sharing all he saw in his.

In a similar way, we open new doors for our child's learning when we share the wonder of our own perceptions and experiences. Suggestions for the upcoming week are designed to help you assist your child to build a solid foundation in math and the sciences—even if they weren't your favorite subjects in school.

1. If you have young children, allow them plenty of opportunities to play with your measuring spoons and cups. Preschoolers enjoy filling things with water and pouring liquid from one container to another. With a small amount of direction, you can encourage them to count how many small cups of water it takes to fill a larger cup. Don't push your child to learn fractions or other complex concepts. Just set the stage for further growth.

   Older children can benefit from a similar exercise—following a recipe. At first they will require assistance, but soon your kids will be able to accomplish this task on their own.

2. Increase young children's interest and involvement with numbers by giving them many opportunities to sort and count. You might begin with colored blocks but switch to a more practical skill like sorting laundry. "Find and count all the black socks, Eric." "Put all the white socks in the drawers, Kelly. Tell me how many you see."

   Show older children how to sort and count money and make change. Working with money creates fascinating and useful experiences with addition and subtraction. Let children handle the money when paying for several small items at the store.

3. To build a positive attitude about mathematics, make learning math concepts a game whenever possible. For instance, playing cards is a good way for younger children to learn sorting, grouping, and sequencing. According to child psychologist Dr. Margie Golick in *Deal Me In: The Use of Playing Cards in Teaching and Learning,* playing cards are particularly helpful because they motivate a child "to work at something over and over again just because it is so intriguing, so challenging, or so much fun."

   Cribbage is an excellent game for youngsters age 10 and older. This game involves many forms of counting, adding, sorting, and sequencing that older children will enjoy. Repeated practice in this game involves exercises in mental math as well as positive interaction between adult and child.

4. The study of percentages is often particularly challenging for children in grade five and beyond. You can assist your child in this skill by offering her the opportunity to see its value in everyday life. Stores typically have products marked down by a certain percentage. Help your child work with percentages by challenging her to find the price difference between a 25-percent, a 30-percent, and a 50-percent discount. This exercise can

be repeated until the child masters the skill.

5. Trips in the family car offer many opportunities to practice skills in map reading, using mileage charts, and figuring miles per hour. Distances can be calculated and miles per gallon computed. Designate a child as the "trip recorder." Give him a notebook to record and calculate information.

6. At the same time you offer one child an opportunity to work with mileage, distances, and gasoline use, you can put another child in charge of trip finances. This child can record all trip expenses, figure average daily expenditures for various items, and keep track of the declining vacation budget balance. Experiences with money and budgeting are excellent ways to underscore the value of math, while teaching the skill of personal finance and budgeting.

7. Ask your child to help you set up a garage or rummage sale. Ask her to price items on predicted market value. Talk about the real costs of advertising and price tags as well as the hidden cost of time spent in preparation, sales, and cleanup. Estimate the possible profit and compare it to the actual total.

One of the primary tools used in science is observation. To help your child develop this tool, try one or more of the following activities.

8. Place a bird feeder in a site easily viewed from a

window in your home. Record the kinds of birds that use the feeder, the time of year they visit, and the seeds they prefer to eat. Use a bird book to help your child identify the birds. Take photographs of birds at the feeder and mount them with written entries in a journal.

9. Plant a garden. Even a small garden grown in large clay pots can help a child learn about seeds, how they germinate, and what plants need to grow. Older children will enjoy growing more than one variety of the same species—different varieties of tomatoes, pumpkins, or sweet corn.

10. Collect and view insects in a screened container. Help your child observe the characteristics of insects by counting legs and body parts. Note shapes and sizes. Are the insects more active in daylight or at night? What do they eat? Where are they most often found? Get a book from the library to help you correctly identify the insects and their body parts.

11. Make a rock collection. You can add to this project for years as you collect rocks from vacation spots around the country. Compartmentalized containers often used to hold screws, bolts, and nails will house a rock collection neatly. A rock identification book is a must for this project.

12. Practice orienteering with your family. Contact your local public library, conservation district, or

area geological survey to obtain a topographic map of your community—or a nearby area suitable for hiking. Teach your child to read a map and compass. Check out books on orienteering at your library. If you have difficulty obtaining a topographic map, contact the United States Geological Survey, Department of the Interior, 119 National Center, Reston, VA 22092.

⚭ Week 4 ⚭

Teachers and Leaders

One of the best things you can do for your children's academic success is to be involved in their educational process. I have detailed many things a parent can do at home, but loving your children and helping them learn also means supporting them at school. Parents of young children are often involved with their children's education through regular attendance at parent-teacher conferences and school programs. Unfortunately, this does not always hold true as children get older. *What Kids Need to Succeed*, a survey of 273,000 students in grades six through 12 in 1989–90 conducted by the Search Institute, found that only 26 percent of the kids surveyed had parents who were involved in helping them succeed at school. This involvement included talking with their kids about school, occasional assistance with schoolwork, and attendance at school events. Unfortunately, nearly 75 percent of the children in this age bracket received no support from their parents in school-related activities. Educational support is vital to your child's well-being. The following suggestions will bolster your parent-school relationship.

1. Attend parent-teacher conferences even if your child is in high school. Take an interest in her work and get to know her teachers.

2. Pray for your children's teachers. Make them a

part of your regular personal prayers and remember them in family devotional prayers as well.

3. Let your children's teachers know you appreciate their efforts. This goes for coaches, advisors, Sunday school teachers, and other kinds of leaders. Encouragement is a powerful motivator and makes everyone feel better. And what parent wouldn't prefer that positive, motivated teachers work with her children rather than ones who are worn out and discouraged?

4. Volunteer to help your children's teachers with class projects, field trips, and other classroom activities. Parent volunteers make a big difference in what teachers can accomplish, and they increase the amount of attention teachers can give to each child.

5. Participate in your parent-teacher association. When your child enters high school, you may serve as a band booster, a choir parent, or a sports club member.

10
EXPRESS LOVE BY SHARING YOUR FAITH

It was a hot night in late August. Condensation trickled down our glasses of iced tea and perspiration dripped down our backs. We had just finished another one of my mother's delicious meals and Dad had gotten up to get the Bible and devotion book out of the cupboard. We three kids sat glued to our chairs, partly from the stickiness of the weather but mostly from habit. My parents insisted on family devotions. Sometimes we kids fidgeted. Sometimes we listened and participated. Sometimes we read the Scripture reference or the devotion.

Now some 24 years later, I couldn't tell you much of what was said that evening. I don't remember what we had for supper. What I do remember was my father praying and the catch in his throat at the close of the devotion. It sounded as if he was choked with emotion. He talked about how this would be one of the last times we would be together. In a day or two I would be leaving home for a college hundreds of miles away. For the first time, I realized he would miss me. He would miss having us all gathered around the table and he would miss our family devotion time. Imagine that! After years of squirming and giggling, yawning and fidgeting, he would miss having me there. And I would miss being there too.

It's a funny thing about sharing faith within the family. Over the years, certain moments and stray comments stand out in one's mind, but mostly it's the pattern, the routine, the example that was established by years of keeping God first. I can't recall much of what my parents said to me, but I can remember vividly what they did.

I remember that when the church doors were open, we were there as a family, sitting in one of the front pews. I remember doing my homework in the church basement while my parents attended choir rehearsal on Wednesday evenings. I remember long rides home in the car, discussing the sermon and events of the service. Most of all, I recall the positive attitude we had about being part of a church-going family. There was never any question about being a part of worship, at home or away. It was something we did with joy and regularity. It gave purpose and direction to our lives.

Studies have shown that healthy families have a mission and a purpose. We believe that as His children, God gives us these two vital directions. As a child, the Holy Spirit established mission and purpose in me through my parents' words and example. I felt secure knowing God had a purpose for my being and a mission for my life. It gave me confidence in living, and in leaving home, even though I would miss my family.

Many of life's most important lessons are caught rather than taught. This is not to say that intentional teaching of our children about God and His ways is not important. Rather there also needs to be an emphasis on the significance of modeling. Children must see us do what we teach. Actions do speak louder than words.

Many of us probably don't give much thought to how we do what we do until one of our offspring starts mimicking our behavior. We see our daughter with her dolls lined up in front of her, speaking to them just as we have spoken to her. We hear our son slamming a door in a fit of anger and wince as we realize we've done the same thing ourselves. How hard it is to remember our children are watching us all the time!

We may long for opportunities to share our faith verbally with our children, but we need to remember that what we *do* as we go about our lives shouts at them all day long. In the days ahead, use these ideas to love your child and your spouse through the sharing of your faith. Trust God to help you walk the walk as you talk the talk.

 **Week 1**

Share Your Faith through Example

1. Read the Bible on a daily basis. Spend time reading the Bible and praying with your husband. Make it a priority to spend at least 10 or 15 minutes studying God's Word. Use a devotional guide to assist you if you wish. Ask your pastor for study guide suggestions.

2. Attend worship regularly—even when company comes or when traveling. Making worship a priority helps your child see the importance of attending church regularly.

3. Attend an adult Sunday school class or Bible study group. Emphasize the importance of continued growth in God's Word by placing yourself in a position for continued learning.

4. Pray! Pray at mealtimes and at bedtimes. Use formal and informal prayers. Pray by yourself and with your husband. Pray with your children and let them know you are praying for them on your own. The example of prayer is a powerful one that will speak volumes to your children in years to come.

5. Speak positively about your church and its leaders. Children can be turned off to the organized church if they hear negative comments from their parents. Every church is filled with imperfect

people. Whatever challenges your church and its leadership face, let your child know you are bringing them before God in regular prayer. Seeing you deal with others in a loving manner presents a good model to your children and honors God as it expands His kingdom on earth.

6. Share your faith with your husband and children. Tell friends about Jesus and His love for them. Children are often encouraged to let their light shine, but they may lack a positive role model for witnessing. Help your child see the importance of sharing one's faith.

7. Practice repentance and forgiveness. We want our children to express their sorrow over things they have done wrong, but the most effective way to teach this habit is to do it ourselves. When you lose your temper, when you wrongly accuse your children of something they haven't done, when you forget something important to them—apologize. Tell them you're sorry. Ask for their forgiveness and express your desire to behave differently in the future. Let your children see you and your husband forgiving one another.

Confess your sins and ask for God's forgiveness in family prayer. We can talk and talk about confession, repentance, and forgiveness, but until we model them ourselves, our words will have little impact on the ones we love most. The Holy Spirit teaches our children powerful lessons through our behavior as wife and parent.

# Week 2

Share Your Faith by Studying God's Word

Study your Bible on a regular basis, and help your child come to know and love God's Word as you do. Take seriously the example of Timothy's mother and grandmother who taught him to know and love the Lord. Your child's age and maturity will determine the materials you use and the time you devote to daily Bible study. But don't wait to get started. Even very small children can be held on a parent's lap as they are reminded of God's love through quiet words, brightly colored Bible storybooks, and simple songs. Use this week's suggestions to help get everyone in your house involved in studying the Scriptures.

1. Choose a regular time to share God's Word with your child. For some, this may be a Bible story before bedtime. Others may choose to have family devotions before or after a family meal. Make it a routine part of daily living.

2. Help young children make pleasant associations between the study of God's Word and special time spent with you. Hold them close as you read to them. Put your arms around them as you pray. Sit on their bed or close by their side as you answer their questions. Remember the words and actions of Jesus Himself when He dealt with children.

3. Change Bible study or devotional formats as children grow. Toddlers will enjoy the Hear Me Read Bible story series and *Little Visits for Toddlers* (both are from Concordia Publishing House). *Little Visits with Jesus* (Concordia, 1995) is appropriate for children ages 4 to 7 and *Little Visits with God* (Concordia, 1995) is written for ages 8 to 10. Older children will enjoy reading and discussing devotional magazines or a study Bible.

4. Help your children apply the Bible to real-life situations. Small children can learn to treat each other with love. Adolescents can search God's Word for answers in learning to deal with life issues, environmental concerns, and human sexuality. Purchase a study guide to assist you with certain topics if necessary. Help your child see how God's Word applies to today's world.

5. Let your children see you and your husband making time for Bible reading and discussion. Consider getting the Bible and devotional materials on audiocassette. Many excellent possibilities are available today and may be just the thing for popping in the tape player during driving time.

6. Use a devotional guide for couples. Start each day, close each evening, or conclude a mealtime with a brief devotion just for you and your husband.

∽ Week 3 ∽

Share Your Faith through Song and Verse

Music has the ability to penetrate the heart when words alone may not. This week's suggestions are designed to help you use the gift of music to encourage your husband and children.

1. Listen to a Christian radio station. Interviews and music can spark discussions about God and His Word with your husband and children.

2. Play Christian music in your home or car. Children learn lyrics easily through repetition. How much better to fill their minds with songs that will strengthen their faith and reassure them of God's love than to expose them only to television jingles.

3. Sing with your children. Have fun learning new songs to praise God. Look especially for songs designed to help children memorize Scripture. These songs make hiding God's Word in our hearts easy to do. *Little Visits on the Go* and *My Bible Stories* (both from Concordia) pair devotions and Bible stories with children's songs in a book/audiocassette package.

4. Plan ahead to help your child memorize God's Word. This is especially important if your child does not attend a Christian day school or is not involved in a Sunday or weekday program that

stresses memory work. Decide in advance what you want your child to memorize during a specific time period. Lay out your plan and then work through it intentionally, helping your child commit portions of Scripture to memory.

5. Learn as you drive and have fun while you do it by using time in the car to memorize Scripture passages. Write the verse of the day or the week on an index card and keep it close at hand. As you drive, work with your child to commit the passage to memory. Younger children can be helped with this task by including hand motions to accompany the words. *My First Bible Verses* (Concordia, 1996) pairs simple finger plays with short Bible verses appropriate for young children.

6. Encourage your husband with a song of worship or praise by purchasing an audiocassette with a favorite song. Set the tape to play at the chosen selection. Wrap your gift with a note to insert the tape in the tape player. It will begin to play with your preselected song. (This can also be done with a CD if you record the number of the musical selection on the card.)

7. Attend a Christian concert. Listen to a variety of traditional and contemporary Christian music. Discuss variances in style and help family members appreciate the many ways we can use music to praise the Lord.

❧ Week 4 ❧

Share Your Faith through Symbols

In *The Christian Family,* Larry Christenson emphasizes the importance of symbols in the way we decorate
our homes. Symbols either dull or intensify our awareness of Jesus. He tells the story of a woman whose three
sons all took jobs as sailors, much to her dismay.
Because she never spoke about seafaring professions,
she could not understand how all three chose this voca-
tion. One day a visitor to her home made the following
observation:

> *"How long have you had that picture?" the
> visitor inquired, pointing to a large painting that
> hung in the dining room.*
>
> *"Oh, for years," the woman replied, "ever
> since the children were small."*
>
> *"There is your answer," the visitor said. For
> hanging on the dining-room wall was the painting
> of a large sailing vessel cutting smartly through
> the waves, its sails at full billow, the captain stand-
> ing straddle-legged on the quarter-deck, his spy-
> glass in his hand, scanning the horizon. Morning,
> noon, and night—with every meal—the boys had
> taken into their inner consciousness the sense of
> high adventure portrayed in that picture. Effort-
> lessly, with never a word being spoken, it had
> planted in them a hankering for the sea.*

Larry Christenson concludes that the surroundings in the home have a tremendous impact on the growing child. This week's suggestions focus on ways you can decorate your home in a way that will foster spiritual growth.

1. Go outside and come into your house as if you were entering it for the first time. What is the first thing that indicates your home is a Christian home? Consider hanging a door knocker, banner, or picture on your door or in the entryway that would witness to your faith in Christ.

2. Take a look around your kitchen. Is there something to remind your family that Jesus is a part of every meal and conversation? Consider adding some item—however small—to reinforce this perception. You may want to keep a Bible and devotional material in the kitchen to help you instill the family-devotion habit.

3. Step into your own bedroom. What would your children see there to remind them that you are a Christian? What evidence exists that you begin and end the day talking to the Lord? Speak with your husband about how you can remind yourselves of God's presence in your bedroom.

4. Now take a peek into your children's bedrooms. What do they have in their rooms that helps them recall God's love and protection? What could you add—a picture, a framed Bible verse, a poster, or a

small statue—to remind them of God's presence?

5. Get your family together and tell them you've been thinking about adding more visual reminders of God's presence to your home. Ask for ideas and suggestions for items to add in the family or living room. Choosing an item together will deepen its meaning for your family.

6. Outdoor flags and banners are popular as seasonal decorations. Buy or make a banner with a Christian message—a nativity scene instead of Santa, the word *Alleluia* rather than the Easter bunny.

7. When you celebrate Christmas, Easter, and other Christian festivals, examine your home for evidence of the true meaning of the season. Ask yourself whether an unbeliever would know your family celebrates the holiday differently by looking around your house. If you find yourself lacking in this area, enlist the help of your husband and children to make or purchase decorations that proclaim your love of Christ.

11

DEVELOP A SERVANT HEART

Bert and Millie invited a young couple home for breakfast after church one Sunday. Bert and Millie's children were grown, and their dinner table was often silent. The young couple from their congregation had moved away from parents and friends. A close bond grew between the two couples as the older pair supported the younger.

Jack and Lois shared their dinner table weekly with a single parent and his son. The man's wife had died of cancer. He and his young son enjoyed the home-cooked meals and lively conversation.

Jerry and Margo volunteered to assist with their church's youth program. They helped arrange retreats, formed relationships with several teenagers, and encouraged the young couple who led the group.

All of these couples knew something important about God's purpose for marriage—the union is for more than companionship and raising children. According to Kevin and Karen Miller in *More Than You and Me,*

Genesis assigns a third meaning to marriage: joint, fulfilling service.

> God placed Adam and Eve in the Garden and said, "Take care of this, you two. It's a big job, and you'll need each other. Together—till, plant, replenish, create."
>
> God has planted this hunger deep within every married couple. It's more than a hunger for companionship. It's more than a hunger to create new life. It's a third hunger, a hunger to do something significant together. According to God's Word, we are joined to make a difference.

Of course, couples aren't the only people who benefit from serving others. Children, too, can learn much by giving of themselves. Dave, Cheryl, their children, and another family cut a load of wood and delivered it to an inner-city mission in their truck. As they unloaded their vehicle and toured the distribution center, their children looked around wide-eyed. A room full of blankets here, shelves full of shoes there, boxes of food everywhere. The director took them to see a family living nearby—a family of eight, all sleeping on the floor in the only heated room in the house. The visiting children began to see how fortunate they were to have food, clothing, and beds of their own. They realized they could help those less fortunate than themselves by working on the woodcutting project with their parents and donating some of their clothes and toys.

Children gain much when they learn to serve others. Family researchers and human behaviorists have noted a preoccupation with self-esteem and self-worth as a phenomenon of the mid to late 20th century. Our culture tends to stress what parents can and should do to raise healthy children rather than what children themselves can do.

One family's answer was to steer a child into a personal servant event. Fourteen-year-old Jesse, too young to drive and not particularly motivated as an athlete or student, moved through his days with little enthusiasm or direction. When summer rolled around, his mother told Jesse he was to volunteer four days a week at a local convalescent home. He was not thrilled with the prospect. Nevertheless, his mother prevailed and dragged her reluctant son off to his first day of "volunteering."

By the end of the first week, a transformation was taking place in Jesse. By week 2 he was ready on time each day and actually looked forward to seeing the residents. When summer ended, Jesse had gained compassion for the elderly and for individuals with disabilities. His sense of self-worth soared as the people he served looked forward to his arrival and praised his efforts. The staff's appreciation of his help further heightened his sense of well-being. Jesse seemed happier at home and his grades improved at school the next fall. He had experienced personal significance through serving.

Jesus said, "Whoever wants to become great among you must be your servant, and whoever wants to be first must be your slave—just as the Son of Man did not come to be served, but to serve, and to give His life as a ransom for many" (Matthew 20:26–28).

Although we are often tempted to view servanthood as a burden, God intends it as a blessing. There is no greater lifestyle than following in the steps of Christ's servanthood. Through serving we learn what it is to be a member of His "team," to experience the selfless love He gives freely. The unexpected blessing is the knowledge that when we become God's hands and feet, sharing His love in practical ways with others, we serve Jesus Himself.

This month's suggestions are designed to help you love your children by nurturing a servant's heart within them. We begin with ideas for practicing the gift of hospitality by opening your home to others. This action emphasizes that all we have belongs to the Lord, including our homes and possessions. Furthermore, it offers opportunities for family members to interact with others who might enrich and inspire their lives.

⌒ Week 1 ⌒

Serve Others through Hospitality

1. Invite a family with whom you are not well acquainted and whose children are comparable in age to your own to your home for a cookout or a simple supper. This might work especially well for a family new to your church or neighborhood.

2. Host a game night featuring favorite board games. Invite singles and couples who are not well acquainted. Help them get to know each other with some mixer activities at the start of the evening. If you are including children, make sure you have activities planned for them or someone responsible for caring for them while their parents are playing the games.

3. Include single adults and single-parent families in your holiday preparations. You might invite a college student to help you color Easter eggs, ask an older adult to help you and your children bake Christmas cookies, or include a single-parent family in preparing for an Independence Day party. Single people without families nearby are often excluded from holiday celebrations and appreciate being part of a family or friendship gathering at this time.

4. Open your home to visiting speakers or missionaries from your church. Include them in your dinnertime conversations and offer them a bed for the night. Practicing hospitality in this way allows your children to learn and grow from others, and it models for your children how Christians share with others.

5. Include neighborhood children in activities that will help them learn about Jesus. One year my children invited friends from the neighborhood to join us in coloring Easter eggs for an Easter egg tree. As we decorated hollow eggs with resurrection words and symbols, we had an opportunity to share our faith with these unchurched children. Later we saw similarly decorated eggs hanging in their homes. Some families find that opening their homes to a neighborhood vacation Bible school is a great way to meet their neighbors and share their faith.

6. Encourage your children—and especially your teens—to invite their friends for meals and other activities. Welcoming young people into your home gives you an opportunity to become acquainted with your child's friends. It also provides your family with opportunities to share your faith. Include visitors in your family prayers and devotions.

7. Open your home for project parties including board and committee meetings. Often these gatherings take place in a church setting. Meeting at your home offers unique opportunities for fellowship. People are frequently more relaxed in an informal setting and may be more open to conversation and faith sharing after the meeting. Meetings at home have the added dividend of allowing you to avoid using a baby-sitter and expose your children to your involvement in ministry. If your kids are old enough to serve refreshments, set up chairs, or entertain other children who have come with their parents, they, too, can be part of the ministry activity.

Week 2

Serve Others within the Church

In our consumer-oriented culture, people often come to church asking what is in it for them. Rarely is their first response, "How can I serve?" Yet much of the work of the church is carried out by volunteers. Churches typically offer many opportunities for adults to contribute time and ability but few ways for children to serve with their parents. If you want to help your child learn to serve in this arena, your example will speak most loudly, but you can also be intentional in serving as a family. The following suggestions will get you started. For more ideas on how to serve as a family in your church environment, talk to your pastor.

1. Be one of the last to leave any gathering that requires clean-up. Encourage your children to work with you as you wipe off tables, put away chairs, or sweep the floor. For best results, discuss your expectations with your children ahead of time and *plan to leave* when the work is completed.

2. Regularly visit an older, home-bound adult from your church and include your children in this activity. Older adults often enjoy seeing young people, and children can learn much from seniors and shut-ins.

3. Volunteer to be part of your church's clean-up day. Include any child capable of dusting a pew,

washing a window, or assisting in some way with the cleaning.

4. Take a meal to someone who is recuperating from surgery or who has just had a new baby. Allow your child to assist you in preparation if he or she is old enough. Take your child with you when you deliver the meal.

5. Periodically help your children go through their clothing, toys, and games to determine which are suitable for giving to others. Help your kids see that all they have is a gift from God. We can care for these things and then share them with others.

6. Look for ways to share your area of giftedness with others. For example, if you are a gardener, share the fruits of your labors—flowers, vegetables, and fruit—with those who don't have a garden. If you possess a particular skill, volunteer to teach someone else. If you have a musical talent, look for opportunities to use that ability.

7. Encourage your church's leaders—pastors and other professional staff members—by offering them gifts of service. Include your child in helping you prepare a meal for a worker in the midst of a hectic, holiday schedule. Offer to baby-sit so a staff person can have a night out with his or her spouse. Have your child join you in mowing your pastor's yard while he is gone on vacation. Little things, done with love, go a long way toward lifting the spirits of a church leader.

∽ Week 3 ∽

Serve Others Close to Home

"No one ever really gives anything away for free anymore." Haven't you heard that comment? Americans today are more skeptical than ever about supposedly free gifts or service. Everything, they think, comes with a price tag or obligation. Perhaps that's why many people have such a difficult time understanding the concept of grace. How could God really give us something when we have done nothing? Nobody does that.

This week's ideas suggest ways to show God's love in practical ways to others—no strings attached. According to Steve Sjogren, author of *Conspiracy of Kindness*, unassuming deeds done by Christians convince more people of the love of God than all the words in the world. When people ask why you're doing what you're doing, say what Sjogren says, "We're doing a community service project to show God's love in a practical way—no strings attached." In every case, refuse to take money in return for the service—smile, and then be on your way!

1. If you live in a wintry climate, get the family up early after the next snowstorm and shovel the sidewalks of people in your neighborhood. Do it regardless of whether they could do it themselves.

2. Rake leaves for your neighbors—particularly

for those who might not be able to do it easily for themselves.

3. Many communities have Meals-on-Wheels, a food delivery service to shut-ins. Volunteer to help with this service on a periodic basis.

4. Set up a lemonade stand with a new twist. *Give away* a cool drink on a hot day as a demonstration of God's love. Popsicles also work well.

5. Arm yourself with plastic trash bags and scour the neighborhood or a nearby roadside for trash. Do this on a regular basis as a gift to your community.

6. Go to a local Laundromat armed with rolls of quarters for washers and dryers. Feed the machines for patrons. Sweep the floor, wipe off the folding tables, and tidy up the facilities while you wait.

7. Offer shopping assistance to shut-ins. Buy groceries, household items, and drugstore items for those who are unable to leave their house to shop.

 Week 4

Serve Others beyond Your Neighborhood

According to the fall 1994 issue of *Compassion Magazine*, children around the world and even in our own country suffer more than adults from the ills of poverty and disease. In Peru, 88 out of every 1,000 children die before their fifth birthday. Health problems in this South American country are often the result of malnutrition, which contributes to respiratory infections, diarrhea, and tuberculosis. In some countries, children are orphaned as the result of war. Even in America, where most children have running water and sanitary conditions, more than 14 percent live in poverty.

If you live in a middle-class community, you and your child may only be exposed to these problems through the evening news. Jesus calls us to care about the poor and needy in the world. The following ideas are meant as springboards to help your family get started on its own mission project. Help your child develop a compassionate spirit and a servant's heart as you reach out with Christ's love to others.

1. As a family, "adopt" a child in a third-world country. Organizations such as Compassion International coordinate such adoptions in which an individual or family supplies support for a child in another country. Pictures of the child and letters are often sent to the adoptive family.

Encourage your children to contribute a portion of their allowance to be part of an important ministry to others.

2. If you live in a rural community, consider coordinating an exchange visit with a school or family in an urban area. Through such an exchange, you will give urban children a look at rural life and your children a taste of city living. Look for ways you can be supportive of churches or ministries in urban areas by talking to your pastor or contacting your church's denominational headquarters.

3. Encourage your teen to take part in a short-term mission project in the United States or in another country. Real-life experiences with missions of this sort can have a positive, life-changing impact on teens.

4. Adopt a missionary family. Pray regularly for the family. Write letters of encouragement to them. Send them cards and notes on special occasions. Look for specific ways to support their work.

5. Collect supplies for a specific world mission project, such as health kits, quilts, or school supplies.

6. Contact a local domestic violence shelter. Determine needs (clothing, toys, personal grooming supplies, blankets) and organize a collection of such items for the center.

7. Contact an area food pantry to learn more about the services it offers and the items it needs. Volunteer to stock shelves, distribute food, or serve meals as a family. Support the work of the pantry in your own community and organize the collection of additional food stuffs if appropriate.

12

BUILD
TRADITIONS

"Read me *The Little Red Caboose,* Mommy! Let's read that one again." Even though my 2-year-old son had heard the story enough times to recite the pages from memory, he wanted to hear the same story nearly every night. Other books held momentary appeal, but most frequently he wanted to hear me read the familiar words of *The Little Red Caboose.*

"On the eighteenth of April, in Seventy-five ..." began my father at breakfast every April 18th. "Do you know what happened today, many years ago?" he would quiz us. Of course he was quoting Longfellow's "Paul Revere's Ride," but it become a ritual for us children. It emphasized our father's love of learning and poetry. It also became our game, a symbol of our family's closeness.

"We can't open our Christmas presents early," our children wailed one year. We had innocently suggested we should open our gifts before we traveled several hundred miles to their grandparents' house for Christmas. "It just wouldn't seem like Christmas if we open them ahead of time," they insisted. "We want to take them with us and open them on Christmas morning, just like always!" According to the tradition we had established as a family, there were certain ways things must be done, and we were not to alter those ways except for an emergency. In their eyes, the logistical problem of stuffing all the gifts in an already crowded vehicle did not constitute an emergency. It wasn't even a problem. We would just be a little "cozy" in the car so we could take all the mysterious packages with us.

From their earliest years, human beings love ritual. According to Leif Kehrwald in *Families and Youth: A Resource Manual*, "rituals provide order, security, and healthy predictability in an often disorderly life." Perhaps that is why we love to sing the same songs every Christmas, sit in the same pew every Sunday, and fly the flag every Fourth of July. We feel safe knowing some things don't change. It's important to have some stability when the world around us feels chaotic.

Ritual and routine form a large part of our lives. They lend order and predictably to our days. We establish traditions for special days and seasons and rituals for rites of passage and noteworthy events. According to Sandra DeGidio in *Enriching Faith through Family Celebrations*:

> *We are natural ritualizers. Our most common-place experiences are ritualistic: parties, parades,*

watching football, conventions, walking the dog, homecomings. Yet we seldom reflect on these as rituals that carry with them deeper meanings about our lives.

God knows the importance ritual has in our lives as a way of reminding us on a regular basis of who we are, where we are going, and what He has done for us. In Exodus 12, God gave the Israelites specific instructions for an annual celebration of the Passover.

> *"And when your children ask you, 'What does this ceremony mean to you?' then tell them, 'It is the Passover sacrifice to the LORD, who passed over the houses of the Israelites in Egypt and spared our homes when He struck down the Egyptians.' "* (*Exodus 12:26–27*)

Celebrating the Passover connected God's people with the work He had done in their lives when He freed them from slavery. It also foreshadowed the saving work of God's Son when He freed us from the tyranny of sin.

When my husband and I married, we were unaware of the impact traditions from our families of origin would have on our relationship. Gradually over the years, as we fought over the ways Christmas "should" be done, we took a closer look at why we each felt so strongly about doing things a certain way. In my childhood home, Christmas celebrations included lots of baking, entertaining, and homemade gifts. My husband's family rituals were a bit more relaxed than my own.

At Christmas my mother and father made choco-late-covered candies to eat and give to friends. Mom baked mountains of Christmas cookies and entertained the entire church and school staff, along with their families. For this event, she decorated our home beautifully, setting festive tables with her best china and silverware. She made hand-stitched and home-baked gifts for every family present. It was a much-anticipated evening for all of us as we looked forward to being with our pastor and teachers and their families. It underscored the value we placed on our church's leaders. To me, it reinforced the importance of hospitality. It said something important about our love for the people God had given to lead and guide us.

The problem came when my husband and I tried to translate this same tradition into our own lives. For one thing, we were in a different position. We were employed as full-time churchworkers rather than serving as active laypeople like my parents. Our Christmas schedules, and those with whom we worked most closely, were hectic. Either we or our colleagues were responsible for church programming, coordinating children's services, and the like. During the month of December, we probably should have simplified our lives, focusing on the worshipful aspects of the season.

Unfortunately, there were many years when I insisted on re-creating the beautiful tradition of hospitality from my childhood in a much less successful way. The result was a lot of tension and conflict as my husband and I tried to manage all the demands of the church calendar along with the demands I was imposing at home. Though I wanted our home to be warm and welcoming during the holidays, it was often cold and uncomfortable for those who lived there because of my insistence on holding to a tradition that no longer fit our lives.

Eventually, after many seasons of stress and tears, I began to release some of my prescribed routines for celebrating the holiday. Together, my husband and I instituted new rituals and traditions that fit our family—experiences meaningful to us and enjoyable for our children. Instead of focusing on entertaining in our home, we took our joy outside our walls as we carried simple baked treats to our friends and neighbors and accompanied the delivery with Christmas carols. Friends often invited us in for a visit that added to our merriment and enjoyment of the holiday season. It was a kind of hospitality in reverse, which worked so well for us that both our friends and our children request the seasonal caroling year after year.

This month's suggestions are designed to help you take a closer look at the routines and rituals of your everyday life. Use these ideas as a tool for constructing more meaningful family traditions.

∽ Week 1 ∾

Day-to-Day Rituals

1. If you don't already have one, begin a morning "rise and shine" ritual with pleasant elements. Play some cheerful music. Spend a few moments sitting on the edge of your child's bed. Give wake-up hugs and kisses as your child desires.

2. Examine your bedtime routine. What pleasant elements does it contain? What could you add to make it a more enjoyable event? Take time to sit on your child's bed for a few minutes and discuss the events of the day. Pray with her and help her leave the events of the day and worries of tomorrow in God's keeping. Read or tell a story and don't forget the hugs and kisses.

3. Familiar routines or rituals are helpful for accomplishing everyday chores. For instance, you might help your child learn to make his bed before coming to breakfast. Or work with your daughter to clean up her work space and gather her homework together in the evening to simplify morning schedules. If children learn to do things in a particular pattern, they will more likely be able to learn to organize their own time as they mature.

4. Most families unconsciously inherit their meal-

time manners from their family of origin. Take some time to consciously look at your mealtime rituals. Who sets the table? How is everyone called to the table? Is the television off during meals so family members can talk freely with one another? How is grace said—everyone in unison, family members taking turns, with a circle of hands around the table? If you like what you see, continue the same pattern. If you'd like to change something or add more positive features, begin now to make some intentional changes.

5. Most families find it helpful to establish an after-school ritual. This might include a snack in the kitchen while you listen to your child's description of the day's events, a review of take-home papers, or time to play before homework or musical instrument practice. Working moms will find it especially helpful to establish a routine for managing the after-school, before-dinner crunch. Setting aside time for this event is reassuring and soothing to everyone in the family.

For Couples

1. Establish a bedtime routine with your husband. Try to go to bed together as often as possible. Share pleasant events of the day. Allow time for snuggling and cuddling before you're too exhausted to care. Pray together and give God the

burdens of the day and ask Him to bless your rest.

2. Scrutinize your rituals of coming and going. Do you part with a kiss and a hug? Do you welcome each other warmly when you see each other? These rituals are often neglected as the years go by, but they continue to be important in reinforcing romance and caring in the relationship.

3. Take stock of your weekend regimen. Is your husband allowed some time of his own without demands and requests from you? Is there time for him to relax? Is relief most needed on Friday night, Saturday morning, or Sunday afternoon? Many couples face conflict simply because they are not in tune with each other's need for rest and relaxation. The husband may want to relax and do nothing on Friday night, while the wife is anxious to entertain. Discussing expectations and needs allows a couple the opportunity to plan a weekend routine satisfactory to both.

⚭ Week 2 ⚭

Rituals for Special Days

When I was a child, we enjoyed homemade caramel rolls on Sunday morning. Getting up early to get ready for church was less of a problem with the promise of Mom's warm, sticky rolls waiting for us in the kitchen.

Family devotions were always the most fun during Advent. We got to light the candles on the Advent wreath and blow them out. Lighting one more candle each week added excitement and anticipation to those dark December days.

We looked forward to rituals at church too. We learned the meaning of the changes of color in the pastor's vestments and the altar paraments and the significance of a somber church on Good Friday and victorious music on Easter morning.

Different colors, particular foods, and memorable practices all heighten appreciation for special days and seasons. Suggestions are given below for celebrating special days common to most families. Use the ideas given here as a springboard for your own commemorative practices.

1. On Sunday mornings, family members need time to prepare their hearts to meet with God. Unfortunately, this morning is often one of the most hectic. Simplify your Sunday-morning routine so the whole family leaves the house in a pleasant

mood. This might include choosing church clothing the night before, getting adequate rest on Saturday night, playing soothing music as you dress, or offering something simple but special for breakfast.

2. Establishing a routine for worship is especially helpful for younger children. This might include talking about expectations on the way to church, getting a drink and visiting the rest room before entering the sanctuary, and sitting where your child is able to see the chancel area. Help your child notice the colors and symbols around the church—especially as they change throughout the church year. Involve your child in the worship experience by helping her find her place in the hymnal, pray with the congregation, and sit or stand at designated times.

3. Take stock of the rituals surrounding your family's devotion habits. Is it time for a change? Are the children old enough to light a candle? Could a different person read from the Bible? How are prayers offered? Setting a regular devotion routine underscores the importance of this practice within a family. Changing it occasionally provides flexibility as family members grow and mature.

4. Celebrate the lesser holidays of the church year in family devotions or with a family meal. This

might mean lighting extra candles on the table for Pentecost or going outside to look at the clouds on Ascension Day.

5. Make generosity a family theme for holiday celebrations. As holidays have been commercialized, the emphasis has shifted from celebrating what we've received to anticipating what we can get. Look for opportunities in every holiday to give something of yourself and your family to others. This might include shared time, possessions, thoughts, or affection.

6. Celebrate baptismal birthdays with a special meal. Include a cake. Light a candle and set an extra chair to remind family members that Christ is the unseen guest at every family gathering.

7. Keep a spiritual emphasis on the more commercialized holidays by adding additional elements to the family worship experience. An Advent wreath is a boost to many families during the holiday season because it adds to their anticipation of the celebration of Christ's birth.

8. Hearts and homes can be readied for Easter through an annual observance of Lent. This 40-day preparation can include using one of many Lenten devotion booklets. Lenten activity calendars can also be purchased for children. Displaying a family-made Lenten banner can also be a powerful visual reminder of the season.

ᴄᴏ Week 3 ᴄᴏ

Rituals for Family Milestones

At 34 years of age, I was nervous about returning to school to do graduate work. It had been years since I'd seen the inside of a college classroom, and I wondered if I'd be able to handle all the academic demands along with my responsibilities as a wife, mother, and part-time employee. My husband expressed extraordinary confidence in my ability, but I wondered several times if I was making the right decision. Would our grade-school-age children be okay in my absence? Would they get to bed on time? Would he help them with their homework? Would I be able to say anything intelligent in class?

My husband must have known my thoughts and fears because he performed a ritual mothers have been doing for years. On the evening of my first graduate class, he carefully prepared a lunch for me, lined up with the children in the front yard, and cheerfully announced, "Wave good-bye to Mom, kids! She's going off to school." I can still remember their giggling faces. They looked like they could handle my absence. I decided maybe I would be able to manage as well.

The ritual my husband performed, sending me off to school with a lunch and his blessing, is one that has given children and parents comfort and confidence for centuries. We need these ways of recognizing rites of passage and family milestones. We need to mark our journey through life with rituals and practices that help us feel more secure. We need the comfort of knowing someone notices we are changing and growing. Use this next set of ideas to help you give more impact to significant events in your family's life and remind you that Christ and His love are the same yesterday, today, and forever.

1. Take back-to-school photos of your children on the first day of each school year. Take another photograph at the end of the school year. (For a special memory, take your children's pictures with their teachers.) Compare the photos and notice the growth and changes.

2. Join your children in a back-to-school prayer. Ask God to bless their school year, their classroom, their teacher, and all their new friends.

3. If your husband is taking additional course work, let him know how proud you are of his efforts. Speak positively of his accomplishments to your children. Encourage him with personal notes placed in a textbook or lunch bag.

4. Celebrate academic progress and success. Make it a practice to post noteworthy papers and art projects. Prepare a special meal to mark the event. Get out the good china. Light candles or use fresh flowers—anything that says, "I'm proud of you. We thank God for your success."

5. Periodically measure the physical growth of your

children by recording their height on a wall, door, or door frame. Pencil in the name and date so your kids can compare their growth with their siblings.

6. Ask a blessing for a family trip or vacation. When the last suitcase is loaded and every family member is securely seat belted in the car, pause for a brief word of prayer and blessing. This positive action can set an important tone for the trip as you call on God to grant peace and protection in travel.

7. Have a bless-our-new-house party. Invite guests to compose and/or recite a prayer, poem, or reading for various rooms of the house. Your pastor may also be requested to give a special blessing for the new dwelling. Ask that it be used as a lighthouse to the neighborhood, pointing the way to Jesus for all to see.

8. Obtaining a driver's license is an important rite of passage that deserves commemoration. Along with all the legal aspects of this activity comes the recognition that one's son or daughter is growing up and gaining greater freedom and responsibility. Rather than dreading this passage, celebrate it with a card, a cake, or a bouquet of flowers. Celebrate your child's first paycheck in a job held outside the home in a similar way.

9. Ask for God's provision and protection when you purchase a new family car.

10. Watching a young person leave home is one of the more heart-wrenching things a parent experiences. Begin preparing for this rite of passage several months in advance by compiling a keepsake scrapbook for the young person, constructing a quilt, or putting together an "emergency love kit" for the days when your child is homesick or lonely. Invite other family members to contribute to the project, which may be modified or simplified for other times when a family member leaves home for briefer journeys, such as a lengthy trip or hospitalization.

Traditions to Mark the Changing Seasons

- We always go to the apple orchard in the fall.
- Dad makes an ice-skating rink in the backyard for us every winter.
- We can't wait to go fishing in the spring.
- Going to the beach is the best part of our whole summer.

Each of these statements reflects a family tradition related to a particular season of the year. Each also tells something about the characteristics of the family—its interests and identity. Healthy families need this kind of "we-ness," this identification of who we are and what we enjoy. A very small smattering of ideas for each season follows. Many more ideas are found elsewhere in this book or in your family's own history and imagination. As you consider the value of tradition in your family's life, don't forget to celebrate the season.

Spring

1. Give a small prize to the first family member to site a robin.

2. Visit a nursery together to choose flowers for planting.

3. Take a drive or walk to view blooming trees and shrubs.

4. Fly a kite.

5. Have a picnic in the yard. Include a family devotion and thank God for the new life He gives us.

Summer

1. Eat breakfast on the deck or patio.

2. Catch fireflies at night and release them in the morning.

3. Make homemade ice cream or visit the local ice-cream parlor.

4. Walk barefoot in the grass, play in the sprinkler, or read a good book on a quilt in the shade of a large tree.

Autumn

1. Visit an apple orchard, pick apples, and drink cider.

2. Rake leaves into large piles and jump in them.

3. Purchase a pumpkin for carving. Save and roast the seeds. If children are old enough to manage the carving themselves, have an annual pumpkin-carving competition.

4. Contribute to a food pantry as part of your family's Thanksgiving celebration

Winter

1. Hold a family contest to guess the date of the first measurable snowfall.

2. Make a snowman, build a snow fort, and have a snowball fight.

3. Build a fire in the fireplace and toast marshmallows.

4. Go Christmas caroling as a family. Take home-made treats to the homes you visit.

5. Choose the Christmas cards you will send as a family. Find ones that will share your joy in celebrating the birth of Chris⸱